THE BEST SEAT IN THE UNIVERSE

A SIMPLE GUIDE TO NAVIGATE LIFE

GRAHAME ANDERSON

This Book edition first published in Great Britain in 2021 by Blue Tao Publishing.

ISBN 978-1-912872-11-4

The Best Seat in the Universe as a phrase is a trademark of Blue Tao Publishing.

Cover Art Tree by Brenda.

❀ Created with Vellum

I dedicate this book to every individual sick and tired of their existing, unacceptable, mundane or repetitive life. Deep down you know by changing you can create a better future for you and your family.

A breathtaking life awaits you.

CONTENTS

AUTHOR'S NOTE

Everyone has a turning point in their life; I suspect you will not be an exception. Your life trundles along as normal until one day you have a realisation. You experience an awakening, a moment of clarity that grabs you by the collar and gives you a good shake. It's in this moment you come to an understanding that your life is no longer acceptable as it is.

This was my experience almost twenty-five years ago. I worked hard as a litho printer, operating print machinery in a factory for over twenty years. I earned money, but barely enough to give me a decent living. My car was old, my house had no carpets and most of the furniture had been given to us. All I wanted was a better life for my wife and me.

As I worked another late shift one evening, my awakening moment came rushing towards me. I wasn't sure quite what had happened to me. I remember standing there, my head reeling and realising my life was a constant repeat day after day. From one month to the next nothing ever changed.

In that moment, I knew something cataclysmic had occurred within me. But what was it? What was different about this moment from every previous one? I honestly don't know, but I recognised one thing: my life had to change.

Not knowing where to turn, a friend suggested the self-help section of my local bookstore. I purchased several life coaching books and devoured them one after another. The advice from these authors was similar: make a plan, create better habits and take action. It all seemed too simple. How was this going to change my life? All the same, I decided if I was going to read what these experts had to say, then I was going to follow their advice.

And so I wrote a plan, adopted new habits and took the first steps towards my transformation. Guess what happened? Nothing. When I say nothing, I mean nothing noticeable in the first few weeks. I continued reading and following their advice. It took another few months then something wonderful happened within me. Small elements of my life shifted. I knew where I wanted to go because of my plan; I felt positive about myself and began to feel I could achieve anything. I was making clear decisions and was focused on where I was headed. Slowly, but steadily I changed. These inspirational books helped me think for myself and instilled within me a new belief. I had more drive and energy after filling up on my daily dose of positive affirmations. The factory worker who'd wasted so much time had left my head and the new me had taken over with bigger aspirations.

My success grew with each new challenge completed, and with my new habits firmly adopted, I became a different person.

Since leaving that factory floor I've run my own business for over twenty years. I'm not successful in comparison to film or rock stars who earn in the super league. But I am in my own small way in terms of where I was to where I decided to be. Over these years I've employed a fair number of people, sold websites and digital marketing services to the value of millions of pounds and enjoyed the freedom of never having to go cap in hand to borrow money from a bank manager for a loan. My success is small but at a level most people would like to achieve.

When I cast my mind back, I realise I would never have lived this vastly improved life had I not made a few simple changes because of that pivotal moment all those years before. I still watch many people I know accepting a poor lifestyle when a better, brighter future lies in front of them. All they need to do is reach out and take it.

So that's my story. What about yours?

Maybe you are barely surviving in tough conditions, trapped in a failed relationship that you can't get out of. Perhaps you want to change career because your employer has passed you by once too often for promotion. Many people's lives go around in continuous circles, and it's hard for them not to feel worn out by the daily grind. And yet, as each new year approaches, you, like many others, probably have simple hopes for your family: you wish for a better life, a little more money, good health and fewer worries. Unfortunately, many people make these same wishes each year and nothing changes. What if, instead of wishing or praying, you implemented a plan of action to propel you forward from where you currently are?

Your reason for wanting to change will differ from others, and that's okay. We all have our own story, our own pains and our own set of circumstances.

My theory is many people stay on the never-ending loop to nowhere because it is easier, regardless of the pain they endure, than it is to want to face change. We know change can be frightening and unsettling, because it's outside of our day-to-day comfort zone.

Is this your moment? Is this the perfect time to shake up your life and get the life you want?

Deep down you know if you don't change your current situation you will be in the same position in five or ten years' time.

How will you feel then if nothing has improved? If you avoid these first steps to a better life, you'll remain where you are, which I suspect is not the happiest place in the world.

Is that the life you want to keep, or do you dream of better?

I'm sure you know change entails pushing boundaries and embracing alternative methods.

I hope by reading this book you will come to a recognition that something has to change, and the best thing, of course, is for it to be you. This self-awakening will be a catalyst for you. Without realising it, by picking up this book you have already taken your first step, which is undoubtedly the hardest. What I want to know is, can you take the second? I'm sure you can. You'll find that each step forward is not as scary as your thoughts – those "imposters" in your head – would have you believe.

And here comes the saddest fact you'll read within these pages. Every person deserves a better life in one way or another, but not everyone wants to make it happen. Business people know success leads to more success. If you can take one step forward, you can take a second and so on. But business is structured and no one tells the ordinary man or woman how to structure themselves for success. Every step away from your old life is a positive step towards a new one. In a year or two you will look back at this moment and not recognise the person who used to be you. Your only wish will be that you had taken these steps years earlier.

Although this is a self-help book, it isn't in the traditional sense. I don't spell out Fifty Ways to Change Your Life or Thirty-Three Secrets Everyone Needs to Know. What I've assembled is more subtle. I venture into short stories to help you relate your situation with Jack, my principal character, and his journey through an unusual world. People remember stories better than rules and to-do lists. Each story within these pages is a prompt to take action in an area if you deem it necessary. Not every chapter will suit you as you will have certain strengths already, however there are chapters that will ring true for you and hopefully focus you in ways you never realised.

I believe my methods can help people find direction to plan their futures in a no-nonsense way. The lessons found within my stories are simple and easy to apply. I'm hopeful you'll find the answers you seek. One last thing: I'd like to set a personal challenge for you as you journey through these chapters with Jack. Like him, I want you to go in search of the Best Seat in the Universe. If you should by chance discover it, you'll understand what being in charge of your life really means.

Grahame Anderson

PART ONE
THE MEETING

ONE

WEIRD, WONDERFUL, TRUE

T he story you are about to read will undoubtedly seem strange. It will sit uneasily in your mind as you try to figure out whether the events discussed could really have happened. You may or may not believe them, and that's your choice. But let me assure you everything reported to me convinced me something truly remarkable occurred.

My name is Frank Cohen, and for thirty years I've written feature articles for the top-selling glossy magazines in the US. I've lived an exciting life with few dull moments and had the privilege to work alongside the power brokers and famous personalities from all sectors, including movies, sports and the political arena. I've been on assignment to most countries and covered frontline stories of tragic events as they unfolded. To say I've lived a blessed life would be an understatement.

However, as some would say, all good things must come to an end, and so after many years of living out of a suitcase my partner gave me an ultimatum: I was to get a job in our home town of Boston or she would leave me.

The high-profile features assigned to me were too involved to cover from my home. I knew my boss would never agree to me working remotely, so I did the respectful thing and gave her my notice.

She's one hard woman. She threw my resignation back before letting me in on a confidential project our publishing house was working on: a new monthly magazine, based right here in Boston. The position of editor was mine, if I wanted it. Junior reporters would gather the raw stories. My job was to fix, edit and publish them. It seemed the perfect outcome for both parties. My boss gave me six months: "Make it happen or we'll close you down."

And so I settled into my new office, as the proud and often embarrassed editor of the strangest magazine on the newsstands: *Weird, Wonderful, True*. A real challenge, especially in this age of everything being delivered online.

Our three reporters were young, keen and full of energy. My position remained as chief sceptic. The reporters loved this weird stuff and would work all hours to meet their deadlines. It wasn't unusual for them to stay up all night trying to take photos of poltergeists or watch witches perform rituals, visit suspected UFO landing sites and interview people who claimed aliens had examined them.

As the months rolled past, our parent company was astounded at the success of our magazine. Our publisher threw more money at us and instructed us to publish fortnightly. While most publications were losing readership, we were growing at an exponential rate.

Those who knew better at head office had a team build a website that rocketed our traffic with story sharing and social media engagement. This was all far beyond me and in many ways I'm glad I can see my retirement looming in the distance. I'm not the biggest fan of allowing readers to comment on every story at the click of a mouse. However, the additional advertising revenue generated demonstrated the value of online interaction.

Boston life was fantastic. I loved its historical past, the excellent restaurants and endless bars set to entice me. My wife enjoyed our newfound togetherness and life evolved into a more settled pace. Having travelled the world many times over, it surprised me how much I enjoyed exploring my home town. I sketched out my future plan to work for three more years and save for retirement, before passing the reins of the magazine to a colleague with grander ambitions.

The morning I first heard of the remarkable story I'm about to tell you began like any other. The phones were quiet, my email contained mainly spam and my team were all out on assignments. I'd been busy editing a ridiculous article about an alien monster encased in the Arctic ice. Some sketchy images of a frozen dark shape accompanied the editorial. As was the norm, there was nothing clear to see, although our graphics department would sometimes enhance these images to assist the reader. My desk phone rang and our youngest reporter, Suzy, spoke at her usual hundred miles per hour.

"Suzy, slow down. Take some deep breaths."

"Sorry, Frank, I got carried away there. Do you have five minutes?"

"Sure, what's happening?"

"I've three projects to complete this week and I can't be in three different places at once."

"What can I do to help?"

"I had a call from a farmer who claims he took a tour to a dimension beyond this life."

I shook my head. "What the hell does that even mean?"

"He reckons while his grandfather lay dying they were connected. Somehow they were pulled into this strange spiritual world together and given a 'behind the scenes' look at life. They went in search of – wait till you hear this – 'The Best Seat in the Universe.' The guy sounded genuine, I promise."

"Genuine!" Frank wondered what was in the heads of his reporters. "Oh, it doesn't matter. What's up with this guy? Why are you telling me?"

"He's on your doorstep, Frank. Brought up and lives on a farm near Danvers."

"I know Danvers, near Salem. In fact, I'm sure it may have been the original Salem before the town changed its name. Please don't let this be a witch thing."

"It's not. I wouldn't normally say this, but this guy sounds plausible. He was going to tell his story to our competitors until I promised him no one less than you would interview him. He knows who you are and likes your work."

"Thanks, Suzy, nice to know I'm in charge of this operation. Send me his details and I'll call him."

"Can't do that. He wants a face-to-face. I said you'd meet him. Remember to take some pictures."

"Can't anyone else go?"

"No, we're all tied up on projects. I hope you don't mind but I checked your diary and said you would be there tomorrow at eleven. I'll send you his details."

Next morning I packed my laptop and a few items into a bag, and grabbed my trusty old Canon. I still preferred a proper camera to a smartphone, especially when wanting depth of field. I'd use my phone to record our conversation or maybe take some video clips.

I drove to Danvers with the full expectation of yet another wild yarn. The reality of my meeting turned out to be very different. This farmer, Jack DeLacey, transfixed me with a story so unique I couldn't do anything other than believe him.

TWO

AN UNUSUAL STORY

D anvers is a pretty "All-American" town nestled in the heart of New England. The last time I visited this area was to study the infamous witch trials of the seventeenth century. Once again, I hoped this wasn't another witch story.

I navigated my way through the small boutique shops to the café, where pastries lined the windows and the aroma of coffee seeped out through the doorway, filling the air. Opposite, an antique bookstore stacked from floor to ceiling tempted me in. Had this been a normal day I could have wasted hours in there, but today I was on a mission. I had to keep focused on the job in hand. My plan was to get a quick outline of this farmer's story, take a few photos and get out, before spending the rest of the afternoon browsing the antique book shop or working on my memoir under some tree by the river.

I found Betty's Deli, our meeting place, which had an open area through the back to a walled garden. The flowers were in full bloom and I chose a table in the corner to avoid being within hearing distance of the other diners. Small birds fought over the crumbs of a sponge cake placed on the bird table. A man dressed in jeans and checked shirt entered and removed his hat. He surveyed the customers and walked up to an elderly gentleman, who shook his head. I signalled to him and he approached my table. He pulled up a chair.

"Frank?"

"That's me." I pulled a business card from my wallet and handed it to him.

"Jack DeLacey." His handshake was firm and had the feel of someone who'd worked in manual labour for many years. I watched him look me up and down as he took his seat. We engaged in polite conversation while waiting for the coffee to arrive.

Experience had taught me never to launch straight into interview questions. My approach was to create a bond between us, get to know the subject better and let them explore who I am. I'd always found I get further with people if I can build a little trust first.

My preconceptions about Jack being a "nut job" appeared unsubstantiated. As Jack told me various stories of his background, he had an honesty about him that seemed genuine. He was hardworking, and his values were not like those I had come across in the pursuit of fame. He was articulate and polite, and focused on what he believed. I liked his ambition and enthusiasm, which burst from him when he discussed his future. Apparently, this was a direct result of his unusual experience.

I'd read so many strange stories since becoming editor of *Weird, Wonderful, True*. Nothing surprised me any more. Most stories had already been told in some form or other with very few original storylines. As soon as someone printed an alien autopsy story, within days another half dozen magazines produced variations on the same topic.

I felt confident in this man and knew he was comfortable

with me. "Tell me your story, Jack," I said. "What do you think happened to you?"

"Not what I think happened to me, but what I know."

"Okay, Jack. I have to ask this one question before we start. The story you are about to tell me, is it the truth?"

"Yes. One hundred per cent. I have no reason to lie to you."

He spoke with a clarity that surprised me. Most of our story clients can act a little stupid. They add details and embellish as they go, but often all they want to talk about is whether they would get any money or a film deal from their story. This man had no interest apart from telling his story.

I placed my smartphone on the table and pressed record. I did my normal intro of who, where and when. "I have with me Jack DeLacey from Danvers, Massachusetts, and this is his story. Over to you, Jack."

Jack cleared his throat and looked around the café. He started slowly at first, and as he gained confidence, his story flowed at pace.

"The reason I have told few people about this event outside of my family circle is I didn't want people to think I had issues," he began. "This happened ten years ago, not long after my twenty-first birthday. I was sure if I mentioned it, people would have me down as some kind of crazy person. I wasn't the brightest at school and thought everyone would laugh at me, so I kept quiet. But ever since this experience I had, I've lived it over and over in my head, and I know I have a story so beautiful I have to share it. People deserve to know what is out there waiting for them."

He had my attention. I couldn't help being intrigued, especially when he mentioned he'd kept quiet for years.

"My grandad lay ill in hospital," Jack continued. "He meant the world to me. We spent most days together working on our farm, fixing machinery, tending the fields and livestock. Everything I know about farming, he taught me. Mum says from the moment I could walk and talk, Grandad took me everywhere. I never felt so close to another person as I did with him. Not even, I'm sad to say, with my own father."

Jack's hands displayed all the evidence of a manual labourer. He was a hard worker, for sure. I understood his sentiments towards his grandfather. Everyone has someone in their life who influences them, maybe a family member or an inspirational friend. I always thought back to my friend's father, who gave me so much guidance, things my own father never did.

"I waited at my grandad's bedside for three days. I knew he might die. I didn't want to consider that eventuality. However, in the event it was to happen, I wanted to be there with him during his last moments." Jack sighed. "For the first time in my life, I noticed how old he looked. Even though he had reached his early seventies, he'd always looked fit and healthy to me. He never acted old. As I watched him lie there I could see how old he was, his face cracked and wrinkled, made worse from years of long hours working outdoors in all weathers. His hands were tough like leather, covered in a multitude of scars from the many times he'd cut them while trapped in the guts of various pieces of farm equipment. He'd even lost the tip of one of his fingers pulling out hay that had jammed and backed up in the baler. He mentioned many times he didn't want to be a burden and said he would prefer to drop dead while working in a field. He made me promise if I ever found him lying in a field I was to prop him up with a pole so he could continue working as a scarecrow. He had a wicked sense of humour."

Tears welled in the man's eyes.

"Sounds like your grandad was a bit of a character," I murmured.

"He was. He worked hard his whole his life until the day he collapsed."

"Tell me what happened, this adventure you mentioned to my reporter, Suzy."

Jack wiped his eyes and blew his nose, catching the attention of some café patrons nearby. "Grandad and I reminisced over old stories of how he got me into all kinds of scrapes when I was young. He said my mother was always terrified he would leave me behind in a field. He never did, of course. As he lay in his hospital bed, I asked him to share his favourite memories with me. And that is when things began to get interesting..."

It's hard to describe my emotions as Jack relayed his story. As I swung from disbelief to delight and eventual understanding, there were times when his eyes filled with tears and I paused my recorder, telling him I would understand if it was too painful, and reassuring him that he didn't need to do this.

The first time this happened, the farmer dragged the sleeve of his checked shirt across the corner of his eyes. "You don't get it," he said. "I have to tell this story. It's not about me or my grandad, it's about a place that exists and yet is unknown to the world. Your readers need to know."

I pressed the record button again. The words you are about to read are Jack's own, verbatim.

PART TWO
THE JOURNEY

THREE

THE BEGINNING OF THE END

"Apart from you and your mother, my favourite memory will always be the big tree," Grandad said, his eyes distant. "If ever something other than human made an impression on me, it was that wonderful tree."

I understood. The big tree had been the favourite place of every child in the district for hundreds of years. No one knew how old the tree was. As far as anyone living could remember, it had always been there. Some said it was four to five hundred years old. Still, I asked him what was so special about it.

"Its size, Jack. No other tree in the whole of New England is that big. It must be four times the size of the next biggest oak tree. The gnarled branches and the thickness of the canopy. The 'den' up a few levels and the rope swings. I loved how the river curved around it and watching the dragonflies zooming up and down just above the water like fighter pilots. To me, it was much more than a tree. So many people made it their hideout, courted their first love and carved their initials into the bark. This was the tree of life. There's something truly magical about that place."

I couldn't agree more. All my life I'd visited the tree, sat under its canopy on the hottest of days, read books and kissed a few girls. Grandad was right: it was something very special.

The nurses had given me a side room adjoining Grandad's, with a makeshift bed to allow me to be close to him. When I knew he was safely asleep, I would try to grab forty winks. The day it happened, I texted my mother to tell her to get some rest and promised to call her that evening. I plugged my phone in to charge, lay down and immediately fell into a deep sleep. I must have been out for a couple of hours when a nurse woke me.

"I think you should be with your Grandad," she said. "His breathing is becoming erratic. It may be time."

I hurried through to his bedside. He opened his eyes and smiled. His voice crackled. A high-pitched wheezing came from him, rising and falling with each breath.

"Jack, my boy, I knew you wouldn't leave me. You and I are always together, like twins."

"Of course I'm here. I had nothing better to do, so I thought I'd drop by." I winked at him.

"I think this is the end of the road."

"Ah, don't say that, Grandad, you're looking good. The nurse said you'll be up and walking and out of here in a few days."

He knew it wasn't true. I couldn't exactly say things weren't looking good, could I?

Grandad swayed back and forth in his bed. Although his voice was deteriorating, he called out his mother's and father's names. I never knew them; they'd both died when I was young.

"They're here, Jack. They want me to go with them."

I began to shake. "Don't go, Grandad, we've still got lots of time ahead of us. You need to get well. I'll do more of the work and you won't have to work as hard any more." Tears filled my eyes, blurring my sight. I tried to hold them back.

"Jack, you need to understand, this is my moment. I want to

go. It's what we all live for." His wheezing got worse. "Mum, Dad – wait for me, I'm coming with you." He stared at me with vacant eyes. His focus was somewhere in the distance, or maybe in his head.

"Please, Grandad, stay a little longer," I pleaded, taking his hand. "There's so much more we've still to do."

The regular beat from his heart monitor slowed. He looked at me and even in his moment of death, he smiled. "Jack, we walked a beautiful road together, didn't we?"

"We did, Grandad. It was the best." A lump formed in my throat that was so painful I could hardly swallow.

He squeezed my hand. "See you again one day, at the next level."

A long tone rang out from his heart monitor. His body relaxed and he looked peaceful. I held his hand tight and told him he would always be with me. Through the window of his hospital room, I watched the medical team rush towards us. And that's when the craziest thing happened.

As I held his hand, I felt a powerful energy like electricity running up and down my arm. With a massive jolt, my spirit, soul, whatever you want to call it, was pulled forcibly from my body. For a few seconds I felt a floating sensation, and everything sounded like echoes in the distance. My surroundings changed from bright hospital ward to pitch black, and then I felt the wind, powerful like a hurricane, buffeting my face. Grandad held my hand as we hurtled through the darkness. He laughed and shouted to his parents, who travelled along beside us. Grandad turned his head. He was laughing until he locked eyes with me.

"No!" he shouted, his eyes widening in horror. "What are you doing here, Jack? Go back, immediately. You can't come with me. This is not for you. It is not your time." He shook his arm, trying to release the grip on my hand.

"I can't let go of your hand," I cried.

He tried desperately to unhook our hands, but we were firmly held together.

"Keep heading towards the light," my great-grandfather shouted, then veered off with his wife in another direction.

We must have looked like comets streaking across the night sky. Up ahead I could see a light. It was little more than a pinprick in the darkness. We flew at speed, closing in on it. It became bigger and brighter the closer we got.

Grandad grinned at me. "This will be awesome. I can feel it."

As we slowed, I noticed there was not one but two lights. Our final descent surprised us by its roughness. We collided with the tops of trees and branches, before thumping hard onto soft ground. We lay still, trying to catch our breath in a blanket of ferns. Grandad and I were no longer joined by our hands.

"This is so strange," he said. "I thought I'd be going through a tunnel of warm light with choirs singing. I was expecting family members welcoming me and angels singing and preparing me for the great almighty."

I knew what he meant. I'd had similar thoughts and felt disappointed for him.

We got to our feet and patted ourselves down. Through the darkness I could see the outline of trees swaying in the wind, lit from behind by the moon. We walked towards the lights.

What we found couldn't have been further from our expectations. There, parked in the forest clearing, with its engine running, stood an old-fashioned bus, the type popular back in the late sixties. It was idling in the darkness with its headlights on. That was the light we'd followed. Instead of heading towards the tunnel of light to take Grandad to heaven, we had stupidly aimed at a pair of bus headlights.

FOUR

GRANDAD'S BUS

We stood before the headlights of the old bus, shielding our eyes. Grandad scratched his head while looking around, trying to get his bearings.

I didn't have a clue where we were or how I would get back home, but somehow I felt good. Everything seemed bright and clear. The blurriness from travelling so fast had dissipated. Minutes earlier, Grandad had been coughing and gasping for breath; now he looked the picture of health. He looked younger, his overalls were smart and he didn't seem exhausted. I climbed the stairs onto the old bus and Grandad took his position behind the driver's seat.

"Where did this bus come from?" I asked.

"It's mine," Grandad said and smiled.

I must have looked puzzled when he said this. He had never owned a bus as far as I could recall.

"I've always had a bus, everyone has one." He grinned. "Including you, Jack."

Our flight through the night sky must have affected his thinking.

"We are all born with a bus to take us through life."

I didn't understand what he meant. He wasn't his usual self. There was nothing normal about our situation.

"Tune into life and find it."

I tried to centre myself. Without a doubt, I could see, feel and smell this bus. I thought about Grandad's claim that everyone had a bus. If this was true, why had I never seen mine?

I asked him.

"Because you've never focused in on it. Most people fail to see theirs because they have no plan to follow. What do you think of mine?"

I loved it. Grandad's bus was decorated on the outside from top to bottom in a 1960s vintage style with flowers and sunshine, peace and love, and a few symbols I didn't recognise. It had a huge gear stick and plate-sized dials on the dashboard. The seats were cherry-red leather and slippery to sit on. Above my head hung a net basket shelf to hold luggage, and hoops hung from a rail for standing passengers to hold. Push buttons were mounted on the edge of every other seat for the passengers to alert the driver when they wanted to get off. My favourite feature, without a doubt, had to be the ticket machine clamped to a bracket next to the driver.

"I like it, Grandad, it's a beauty." I turned, and was startled to see several passengers sitting quietly behind us. Some appeared transparent, almost ghostly. "Who are these passengers? Why are they on your bus?"

"Don't you recognise your own family and friends? When they heard I was in hospital, they thought I needed help. So they've been praying and sending me thoughts; that's why they're here riding along in my bus. They feel close to me when they are sending messages of love."

I looked closely at the passengers and realised I did recognise most of them.

Grandad adjusted the mirror. A driver's hat was hanging on

a hook next to his seat, and he reached over and put it on. He revved the engine and put it into gear.

A woman in a long silvery dress appeared at the door. Grandad stepped out from behind the steering wheel. "Hold on, Jack, I need a few moments. Maybe she's my guardian angel." He grinned as he left the bus.

I watched this silvery glowing figure as she reached forward to hold Grandad's hand. They were deep in conversation. I couldn't hear what they were saying. I moved closer to the door.

"Why did you bring someone with you?" the figure said. "You know this place is only for those we call. Your grandson still has a life to fulfil."

"I didn't bring him. We couldn't separate as our hands were locked together. I told him to go back, but he couldn't let go."

"He has to go back. He's not due here for a very long time."

"How do you suggest I get him back? Can't you wave a wand or something?"

"This isn't a magic show, sir. We're not sure how to send him back. It's usually only a one-way ticket in. What you've presented us with is a very rare event."

"Sorry, I didn't mean—"

"It's okay. We're going to help him get back, but it may take some time. What we need is for you to give him a guided tour while we work on an alternative plan. Let him get a glimpse of a behind-the-scenes-of-life tour."

She leaned over and whispered in Grandad's ear. I couldn't hear what she said. As she stepped back, a golden aura projected from her and she waved to him.

"Help your grandson find the Best Seat in the Universe," she said.

"Are you sure?" Grandad asked her.

She nodded.

Grandad stepped forward to hug her, and she disappeared

into a few wisps of light flying off into the night. After staring after her for a moment, he turned to see me in the bus's doorway. "Did you hear what she said, Jack?"

"Only the bit she didn't whisper." A strange feeling twisted in my gut. "All I want to know is how they are getting me back to the hospital."

"Don't worry, they have a plan," said Grandad, taking his position in the driver's seat again. "In the meantime, we're going on a tour."

"But you don't know where we are!"

"That's what you think. You're forgetting I have my bus. I'm taking you to the most important place you will ever visit."

"And where would that be?"

"We are going to find the Best Seat in the Universe."

"The what?"

"You heard me. And when we find it, your life will change forever."

FIVE

A TICKET TO THE BEST SEAT IN THE UNIVERSE

We left the forest, our bus jostling over the rough ground.

Questions flooded my mind. "Won't someone miss this bus? We shouldn't have taken it. It's not ours."

"I told you, Jack, it's mine."

The smell of the red leather seats mixed with engine oil reminded me of the ancient tractors we'd driven around the farm. We'd only been moving for two minutes when a woman pressed the button to get off. Grandad stopped the bus.

She held his arm. "You'll be fine," she said, and stepped off.

The bus felt weird, almost dreamlike, and yet Grandad assured me everything was real.

"Where we are is on the edge of life. We're on the other side, on a different wavelength or vibration. We can no longer see our old world and they can't see us. Things will become clearer soon, I promise."

"But I'm trying to figure it out. Why a bus?"

"It's straightforward, son. A bus takes you from one point to another. From the start of your journey, at birth, to the end, at death. It's your unique journey. You see places, meet new people and some become friends. They step on and off your bus as your paths cross through the years. Your family is on your bus daily and you are on theirs. A relative may move abroad, so they get off at a crossroads and their bus heads in a new direction. You may not see them for years, then one day they arrive back on your bus. That's how life works. People come and go all the time, and you never know for how long."

"Are you honestly saying people can get on and off my imaginary bus at any time?"

"Yes, but it's not imaginary, it's real. The people who surround you have come and gone on your bus since the day you were born."

It was so confusing. What Grandad said made sense, but I'd never seen my bus. I asked him why.

"Your bus will appear when the time is right. You know it's there already, but you still have to seek it out. When you find it, you'll realise all the opportunity it brings. You'll be able to steer your bus and take control. You'll define goals, then point your bus towards the life path that you choose. Does that make sense?"

"It sounds right. But what if I can't find my bus?"

"You will, Jack. Without a bus or a plan, you have no direction."

I realised there must be some kind of truth in what he said.

Grandad adjusted his driver's hat and leaned over his ticket machine. He cleared his throat and adopted a posh voice. "Where to, sir?"

"I'm happy to go anywhere."

"Anywhere is nowhere, son. Be specific if you want to hit your target."

"I'm not sure."

"That's fine. It's okay to take your time and plan where you are going. In the meantime, we'll go in search of that special place." He turned the handle twice on his ticket machine. A small lavender-coloured paper ticket slid out the bottom. In bold type it read:

DESTINATION: THE BEST SEAT IN THE UNIVERSE

"Is this where we're heading?" I asked.

"Not immediately. It will be our ultimate destination. I think we should make this journey more exciting and stop at a few memorable places along the way."

"Good idea. I'll call Mum and let her know." I reached into my back pocket then realised I'd left my phone charging in my room at the hospital. "I can't contact her. Maybe we should head back to the hospital, they'll be missing us?"

"Not at all, they'll be busy. You can tell them you wandered off to have some time to yourself." Grandad reached above the windscreen and opened the hatches to the destination board. He grabbed the handles and wound them around, changing the bus number. He stopped it at the number twelve. The second screen he turned slowly around watching all the destinations on the roller blind.

I looked at where he'd stopped:

SIMPLE STEPS TO A BETTER LIFE

SIX

YOUR BUS CAN TAKE YOU ANYWHERE

We headed down the road, excited to be on our way. The landscape kept shifting from dreamlike to pin sharp. Time also seemed to change so much that I stopped looking at my watch. One minute we were travelling in daylight, then without warning it would change to darkness.

"Grandad, where did your bus really come from?"

His face was beaming as he drove. He lifted his hat and wiped his brow with his sleeve, swerving to avoid a tree, then turned onto a busy highway. "I told you, we are all born with our own bus. Although, most people never find theirs."

"You mean like me? I've never seen mine."

"Look how many there are." He pointed to the bustling highway lanes. "Every bus you see represents a person. Yours may be invisible for now, but believe me, it will appear when the time is right."

Buses of all shapes and sizes filled the highways and side streets. Modern coaches battled for space against old rusting buses. Quite a few were in a terrible state of repair.

"When do you suppose that will be?" I asked him.

"Usually when you make a positive life choice. It's a beautiful moment when you realise nothing can stop you from doing what you want, no matter what obstacles are in your way. It's then your bus will be ready to take you to where you want to go. There are no limits!"

"I sure hope mine appears soon."

"Understand your bus is not a means of transport to take you to physical places; it's far greater than that. It takes you through life and can help you pass exams, learn an instrument, anything you want to aim for. Your bus is there to help you reach your goal."

"Pass an exam with a bus? That sounds ridiculous."

"I suppose it does, but passing an exam is like any goal you aim to achieve."

"In what way?"

"If you can see your goals as destinations, you can simplify your life. Think about this. Everything you do has a series of steps from beginning to end. Each step leads to the next until you complete your task."

"Sounds straightforward enough."

"It is. Let's say your aim is to pass a maths exam. You set your destination board on your bus to *PASS MATHS EXAM* and then you plan your bus stops."

"Bus stops?"

"Of course. If you are driving your life bus, what else could it be? Stop one, buy a maths book. Stop two, attend maths class. Stop three, study hard. Stop four, get help from a tutor. Stop five, revise with sample exam sheets. And at the last bus stop, sit the exam. It's that easy! If you plan your stops, you can work it out."

"You make it sound straightforward, but what happens if I fail the exam? What then?"

"Good point. You either pass or fail, that's life. If you pass, that's wonderful. If you fail, don't panic: repeat the necessary steps until you get it right. Failure is a normal part of success."

"I get it, Grandad. Your explanation seems simple."

"The best things always are. Everything you do is nothing more than a series of bus stops. Try to see your goals in this way. Plan every journey, write your list of stops, before heading toward your first stop. It's always the hardest one, due to the momentum needed to move forward. You could be an astronaut, Jack, the president of the United States or a millionaire; anything you want is there for you to choose in your life. As long as you follow the fundamental rule for any goal."

"Which is?"

"You must really want it."

"But ... but you said I could be a millionaire, become an astronaut, or the president. It all sounds far-fetched to me."

Grandad let out a long sigh. "The world is full of millionaires. It's not that big an achievement."

"I thought achieving wealth was a major aim for so many."

"It is. But many millionaires also work a regular job, even though they don't need to."

"Why would they do that?"

"Because money alone doesn't bring satisfaction. It's labour and creating things you love that bring genuine joy. Never lose sight of your dream, Jack."

"What about being an astronaut or president?"

"Do you think our president at your age ever thought he would be in the White House? Did Neil Armstrong plan to walk on the moon as a young man? I suspect not. Both men came from ordinary families and achieved the highest positions in society. Why not you? Why are you so different?"

"I suppose I never thought it possible."

"That's the problem, Jack. People don't think they are good enough and give themselves limitations. Don't hold back, decide what you want and set up your bus stops. Never lose sight of your dream."

Grandad was right. As the bus rattled along the highway, I tried his method to see what quick plan I could come up with should I decide to be an astronaut.

I would set my destination board as follows:

DESTINATION: BECOME AN ASTRONAUT

First Bus Stop: Find out from NASA what qualifications are required

Second Bus Stop: Study the required subjects and sit the exams

Third Bus Stop: Apply to the astronaut programme

Fourth Bus Stop: Keep trying until I get through the door

SEEING the bus stops in my head made planning seem easy. I could see how it made sense to picture my bus stops as steps towards a destination.

I tried the same formula for the president's job, although it was certainly not a job I would ever want.

DESTINATION: BECOME PRESIDENT

First Bus Stop: Join political party that shares my beliefs
Second Bus Stop: Work hard for the community
Third Bus Stop: Become a candidate at local elections
Fourth Bus Stop: Push for promotion at regional level
Fifth Bus Stop: Run for office

.   .   .

I<small>T WAS</small> a simplistic approach and I could see getting the first step in place was crucial. Planning the rest of my bus stops gave me a clear vision. I was getting the hang of this. I was convinced using my bus stops would help me plan better goals.

Grandad cleared his throat. "You may never be the president or an astronaut. But I guarantee you won't get anywhere if you don't plan your destinations and drive towards them. When you move in the right direction, the possibilities become more real. If you want to achieve something, set your destination goals, plan your individual stops and take action."

"I wish I could see my bus, Grandad. I want to use it."

He laughed. "Patience Jack, I haven't told you yet how your bus can take you in the opposite direction from what you want."

I hadn't been expecting that. "How's that possible, if I set up my stops?"

"Setting too many destinations at the same time. Too many stops, distractions that overlap and waste time until you can't remember where you were heading. Focus on completing one thing before going for the next."

He was right. I had so many unfinished jobs on the farm. Most were half done, and it was hard to decide what to do sometimes. I needed to take control when I returned.

"What results would you expect, Jack, if you half-heartedly studied for your maths exam?"

"Half the marks, I suppose."

"Spot on. If you don't follow clear steps to your destinations, you won't get the results you want. Focus is the key ingredient. Most people have the potential, but don't always succeed. It's also important to know when to ask for help to complete a task. Achieving a goal isn't one big thing: it's good planning and lots of small steps."

"Small steps?"

"Yes. Simple, tiny steps all in a row will take you anywhere you want. If you can keep one hour aside every day and use it to forward your goals, you'll achieve many things. Just one hour a day. Use every minute wisely and don't waste time. Sit at the front of your bus and make your life as exciting as possible."

My head was spinning. I was desperate to take charge of my bus and start moving.

Grandad reached up and changed the destination board:

SIGNS OF LIFE

SEVEN

SIGNS OF LIFE

We drove through the night towards a glow on the distant horizon. Grandad promised I'd learn things about life I wouldn't believe. I have to say that even at my age I could barely contain my excitement.

The headlights cut through the darkness that seemed to swallow the road in front of us. An enormous shape stood at the roadside. Grandad stopped, his headlights fixed on the massive structure. At first glance, I assumed it was a giant redwood tree; the type often pictured in *National Geographic* where you see a car drive through the middle. We stepped off to inspect it. Towering over us was a massive signpost with thousands of signs jutting out in every direction. A small pole stood next to it with a plaque stating, *Signs of Life*.

"Isn't this the signpost to end all signposts, Jack?" Grandad said. "It's such an outstanding example of how confusing life can be."

"In what way?"

"This signpost shows what it's like inside many people's heads. It shows you how they think. It's chaotic: too many destinations creating confusion and clouding their decisions. We at least have our ticket and a plan to our next destination. Many people have too many options and will always struggle to see through the chaos. They need to simplify their lives."

"Maybe it's because they're under so much pressure."

"That's true, but if they can simplify their goals, their lives become easier. Write a basic list, put things in order of importance, and tick each item off one by one. Less confusion and far more achieved." He cocked his head, looking up at the signpost. "Let me show you. Pick six important signs, son, ones that make sense for you, then place them here on this smaller pole."

I looked at the signs. He was right; there were so many. Arrows pointed in every direction, spelling out *Mum's decision*, *teacher's choice*, *relatives' advice*, *own choice*. Signs with places that meant everything to me: home, the big tree, agricultural shows, towns and cities. I picked my signs and placed them in order from top to bottom.

Go to night school
   Learn to drive the harvesters
   Become farm manager
   Travel the world
   Get married
   Build my dream home

GRANDAD APPLAUDED. "Well done, doesn't that feel better? The confusion over there, compared to your signpost, is plain to see. That's how it should be. You can add or subtract when you need to. It's best to have fewer signs, as it creates less confusion. When you complete each goal, remove the sign and add a new one. Simple."

I felt pleased with my choices, as if I'd achieved a life plan.

"Look how easy your signpost is to follow," Grandad continued. "And that's with only a few minutes planning. With each sign picked ask yourself, 'Does this feel true to me?' If it doesn't fit with you instinctively, the wrong decision is being made."

"How would I know?"

"You'd be unhappy. You'd be living a lie to please others. All you do in life is an exciting adventure, the best gift ever – please don't waste it. Every part of the experience should be pure. Only you have the power to shape it the way you want."

Grandad's explanation clarified many things for me. I paced around the post and came to a stop. A sign lay on the ground with *Make your own choices* printed on it.

"I'll take this."

Grandad smiled. He patted me on the back as we walked back to the bus.

As I stood on the steps, I looked towards the horizon. "Where to next, Grandad?"

"Forward son, always forward, if you want the best life has to offer."

"Let's go find the Best Seat in the Universe."

"Patience, Jack. Remember, small steps. Let's visit a few interesting places first. You'll like the next stop."

"Where are we going?"

"To a place that will help you understand your successes and failures."

I was getting the hang of setting a destination. It was so simple and yet something I'm not sure I had been doing with my life. I watched as he set the board once more:

THE VALLEY OF HOPE

EIGHT

THE VALLEY OF HOPE

For over an hour, Grandad drove through beautiful countryside, passing hedgerows lined with wild plants of every kind. Vibrant flowers flourished, their colours spilling onto the grass verge by the roadside. In the distance we could see waves breaking against dark rocks, their foam thrown into the air before crashing back on shore. Cliffs towered along the coastline, leading inland before breaking out into a mountainous area where it was just possible to see cows grazing on higher ground. The mountains stretched for miles, their snow-capped peaks reflecting a pinky-white colour from the sun while clouds crossed over, casting dark shadows that rushed across the hillsides. It was a humbling sight.

"What are you expecting to find in the Valley of Hope, Grandad?"

"A variety of things. This place changes lives more than any other. It's where dreams unfold, and the aspirations of the world are sown for anyone who ever dared to dream. Everything people want, every hope, every dream, starts from here. It's such an incredible place."

Grandad turned off the highway onto an uneven country

road. The passengers held on tight as the bus jostled them from side to side. We could hear the sound of the waves crashing on the rocks blown down by the icy wind from the mountains. Between these two harsh landscapes, the Valley of Hope sat nestled in the middle. Rays of sunshine broke from between the clouds, lighting up the valley.

The bus bumped its way over the last few hundred yards, stopping beside the remains of a campsite. Grandad pulled on the handbrake and requested everyone stretch their legs. The passengers shuffled off and stood in awe at the majestic view before them.

I stepped onto the grass and took a deep breath of the fresh mountain air. This place had such inherent positivity that it made my head spin. We took in the views as sea air filled our nostrils. The valley itself resembled a different world, filled with small rivers and trees, with the sun breaking through silver-lined clouds, its light reaching the ground in great shafts.

To our right, the mountains loomed stark against the corn-flower-blue sky. Forests clung to the steep hillsides. Lower down, green pastures swayed in the wind as herds of cows and goats headed towards fresh, unspoiled grass.

"Can you feel the energy, Jack?"

I could. My body was buzzing, and I was sure electricity was coursing through my veins. I'd experienced nothing like it and was sure I never would again. It was positive and over-whelming.

"I feel fantastic."

Grandad nodded in agreement. "That's the power of posi-tive energy. Enjoy it while you can. You're in a euphoric state because the valley is positive. Those jagged rocks, however, bring a sense of darkness."

"Darkness? In what way?"

"This is the land of hopes and dreams. When people try

new things, they often fail and it's here these broken dreams fall and crash onto those rocks."

We walked along the coastal path towards the rocks that stretched far into the distance. Strewn all around were millions of items. I asked Grandad why there was so much litter.

"It's not litter. This is people's projects, their hard-earned work and broken dreams. All the failed ideas that they started with hope in their hearts but never quite completed for whatever reason, lie here."

We walked among the items, stopping to inspect what lay on the rocks. It was a sorry sight. I looked through the many items, finding songs, half-written novels, poems and letters in their millions, their ink blotched and running off the pages. Inventions lay dashed against the rocks, discarded and broken. I picked up a book and read a poem. A lover's heart-wrenching account of their inner feelings. It was beautiful. Red lines struck through the text and a cross with *Must try harder* written at the bottom in somebody else's handwriting. I felt sick. The cruel words churned my stomach. A dark, heavy cloud of negativity made its presence felt. It was overwhelming.

"I'm leaving, Grandad. I can't handle all this rejection."

We scrambled over more rocks, stopping again to assess more failed dreams. The pain was visible, written into the letters attached.

I fought back tears for every person whose failure lay before me. Was it possible the judges of these works understood how life-changing their comments would be to the creators?

A loud crack of thunder brought me back to my senses. Thousands of items rained down, some hitting us.

"What's happening?" I cried.

Grandad put down the letters and other items he was reading through. He looked up at the sky and raised his hands.

"More failures, Jack, it never stops. Every minute of every day, these dreams fail and fate brings them here."

"I don't get it. To me, many of these things are good enough."

"Many are, but not all of them. They've either been judged as failures or trashed by their owners. That's why they fall here, broken, unfinished. The fire each creator once had in their belly has died. When you experience failure, don't fret. We all have far more failures than successes in our lifetime. For everything we succeed in, we fail a few times first. Look in front of you. The best brains who ever lived are represented in amongst these rocks, probably many times more than the average man."

It was disheartening to see so many dreams being smashed onto the rocks. Love letters, inventions, unfinished works of art, all destroyed. Items burned where they lay, others in shreds; large words scratched across them in red ink: FAILED, UNSUCCESSFUL, REJECTED. Harsh words stamped on these works in mere seconds. It was a savage cruelty that would weigh upon the creator's minds for a lifetime.

I felt nauseated and wanted to run from this place.

"Jack, see this place for what it is. This valley is the most painful learning centre for people. As well as destroying ideas, it also helps to create them. These rocks can elevate the ordinary person into the extraordinary."

"I don't know how you can say that, Grandad. Have you read these letters?"

"Yes, I've read some and empathise with the creators of their work. Every person has hopes or dreams that don't materialise. If you looked amongst these rocks, you would find shattered dreams of mine. Thomas Edison's first failed attempt at the light bulb will lie here in these rocks. Steve Jobs's first computer will be here, as will many other top scientists' inventions and artists' first efforts. It's among these rocks you learn the harsh lesson of what is wrong. You study your work, see what needs to be adjusted and then try again. Every failure encourages a new process of learning to improve."

As we walked from the rocks over to the valley, the darkness lifted and I began to feel calmer. I stood there, taking a breath, and found a moment of peace within the turbulence. We approached the foot of the mountains. The wind swirled and blew leaves around us in circles. Carried on the wind we heard voices, similar to a cheering crowd. It was a strange place, but comfortable. The closer we got to the hills, the more positive my mood became.

Again, items were falling and landing all around us, but this time they looked pristine. They formed a new lush and fertile mountainside. Everything we looked at had large positive ticks on them. *ACCEPTED*, *PASSED*, *SUCCESSFUL* – words of hope spread across the grassy slopes.

I opened some envelopes filled with success stories. Purchased your first home. A beautiful baby boy. Passed exams. Invention accepted. We have hired you. Passed driving test. Thousands upon thousands of completed achievements and dreams added to the mountain range.

"Jack, the ideas dashed on the rocks are an everyday part of life," Grandad said. "With the right attitude, these dreams can transform into success. The people whose ideas fail upon those rocks will find solace again in the Valley of Hope, the middle ground between success and failure. The Valley of Hope is a secure place where we must always return after success or failure. It's where we regain our bearings. In the valley, creators can regroup and analyse what worked and what didn't. This is their opportunity to replan and try again, each time making another slight change."

"What if they can't? What if the failure is too much for them?"

"They may hit the rocks more than once, but each time they learn something new and take another step closer to success. That's what makes the Valley of Hope in all our lives so important; it's filled with positive energy. Hope is a positive energy that gives us the will to push on. Anyone can refocus and try again. These mountains of success make it worthwhile for those who do."

"I get it, Grandad. Understanding failure recognises a step towards success. Acknowledging this makes it easier to try again rather than to give up."

"That's exactly right. Edison created over one thousand versions of the lightbulb before it worked. He didn't see failure; he said it was an invention with a thousand steps to get it right. One last step was all it took, and thankfully it became shared knowledge and all humanity benefited. Edison lived on those rocks for a long time. Imagine how he felt. But he didn't let failure rule his life. He returned to the valley, to his centre, regrouping, rethinking his invention, trying new ideas until one day he reached that mountain."

"I feel more positive now I understand failure better."

"That's good, Jack. Live your dreams if you can please and understand they are not the privilege of the young. Age is no limitation. If people are alive, they can dream. But they must take action."

"What kind of action?"

"Any action that brings their dream another step forward. Most people daydream and don't back their dreams with an action plan. If you are gifted a dream, get on your bus and set your stops towards that destination. Lying on your sofa thinking about it isn't good enough. That's where many of the dreams on those rocks come from. People who took little or no action and gave up too early."

"I have so many things I want to do, Grandad."

"That's good, Jack. Put your ideas into your action plan. Tick them off and add more."

"I will. I'm heading towards those peaks."

We looked at the mountains. As more items fell from the sky, the mountains grew more substantial from the success.

"How much higher can these mountains grow?"

"There's no limit, son. Every person can achieve great things; all they need is a good plan and to act upon it."

"I'm glad we visited the Valley of Hope."

"Me too, it's such an inspirational place. Anyway, we'd better get moving. If you think this place is incredible, I need to show you a roundabout so different from anything you've seen before. It's a real eye-opener."

We left the valley feeling hopeful. We'd witnessed a special place where despair and happiness existed side by side. I now understood they were both necessary parts of any creation and had to coexist in the name of improvement and achieving goals.

I looked at the destination Grandad had set:

THE BIGGEST ROUNDABOUT

NINE

THE BIGGEST ROUNDABOUT

I relaxed as Grandad navigated his way through the heavy traffic. After twenty minutes, we noticed all the buses had slowed to a standstill. A sea of brake lights snaked into the distance. We crawled along at a snail's pace, then took a slip road off the highway. We wove through traffic, our bus climbing a steep hill. As we turned the brow of the hill, the roundabout came into view. Roads merged into it from all directions. Grandad's bus crept forward, eventually joining more lanes of traffic.

"Why have so many people come here?"

"Indecision. They travel their lives in circles. Many who arrive here will never leave. They find a strange comfort in being here."

"Why would they stay on a roundabout? It must be possible for them to get off again."

"It is, but getting off is hard for them because they have to want to leave. They think because they're moving forward that it's positive. They are going around in circles, to nowhere. Unless they decide on a destination, even a wrong choice, they can't leave here."

"Taking a wrong choice doesn't sound smart, though."

"It's not, but it's a decision. Even wrong decisions take you to fresh places. In the Valley of Hope, wrong decisions fell on the rocks. Learn from them and try again."

"It would make more sense if they made a right decision, wouldn't it?"

"It would. But they have to make a choice. To go forward in any direction, right or wrong, is far more desirable than not moving at all."

"So why do they come here?"

"All kinds of circumstances. They feel powerless, lost, and they don't know what to do next. Some unfortunates among them might stay here for life while others will come to a cross-roads, a point of understanding within themselves, and realise they are on a road to nowhere. They understand there's more to life than doing nothing, and so they create a plan. Once they have a plan, they're already moving off the roundabout to a brighter future."

"I don't imagine I'll ever be on the roundabout."

"Never think that way, Jack. Even the strongest among us can end up here. It only takes a few things to work against them before they struggle to cope. It becomes hard to make sensible decisions under pressure. They surrender themselves to their fate and let the comfort of the roundabout take over. It seems like a simple choice for them, but it is not. The power of this place draws them in. They get state aid and don't have to think for themselves. This way of life gives them a false sense of security and once sucked in, it removes their ambition and ability to make their own decisions. They become more vulnerable and have no desire to leave. They know this is not the best place to be, but they adapt and learn to live here. Once their decision-making has left them, it's easier to stay motionless with no direction."

"That's not a good life for anyone, Grandad."

"I agree. That's why I say you have to keep moving forward and choose a direction, even if it's the wrong one. All it takes is a positive decision to bring anyone off the roundabout and back onto a road of discovery. Once they move again, they can work out a new direction."

"I get it. Let's go on the roundabout and see what it's like."

"No, Jack. Why would you want to? We need to avoid it. I'll skirt around the edge and come off at the next exit."

"Avoid it? Come on, Grandad, you told me this is the biggest roundabout in the world. It would be a shame not to go around at least once."

Creases appeared between Grandad's eyebrows. "Jack, it's too controlling. It's hypnotic and will try to suck us in. It seems like a simple answer to life's problems."

I frowned. "How big is this roundabout?"

"Last I heard it was hundreds of lanes wide and miles long and growing."

"Whoa, that's big. You said the roundabout can't control people who decide. We know how to do that."

"I know we can, but what if the people stuck on the roundabout try to persuade us to stay?"

"Why would they do that?"

"Because they want to persuade everyone to stay!" Grandad shook his head. "They want you to lose your will and passion for life and sit with them, discussing how wrong the world is. It comforts them if they persuade others their lifestyle is best. They convince poor unfortunates not to waste their lives working nine to five. Like a vortex, they suck others into a wasted life."

"Why don't they make better choices and leave the roundabout? They don't have to listen to the negativity or stay."

"That's my point." He closed his eyes for a moment and

massaged the bridge of his nose. "They should be able to leave again, but they can't. They live in hope of being rescued. But hope is never good enough, nor will it ever take them off this roundabout. Unfortunately, many of them are here not because they want to be here but through sheer bad luck, or they don't know how to plan their lives. Only a plan with action can move them forward to a better future. And no one teaches us a plan."

"Let's go around once. It will be exciting."

"I think we should avoid it, Jack. I was on here many years ago," said Grandad. "It took me months to get off again."

"One loop, Grandad. It can't do us any harm."

Grandad eased his bus onto the roundabout filled nose to tail with buses. We pulled in and followed behind an old rusting bus. Another came alongside, so close to us we were almost touching.

"Watch him, Grandad, he'll bump into us."

"I see him. His steering is dreadful."

Grandad swerved off to a lane closer to the centre. Buses surrounded ours, many of them in a poor state of repair.

"They're a sorry sight," Grandad said. "It looks like these drivers have given up on themselves. All they care about is food and sleep. No ambitions or life goals."

A bus moved alongside us, the driver leaning against the window.

"Watch him, Grandad, he's asleep, and his bus is still moving."

"A lot of them are. Sleepwalking through life in a hypnotic state."

"Hit the horn and wake him up. He'll bump into us if you don't."

"He might, although if he doesn't hit us, I suspect another will. They need an awakening, but a toot of the horn won't do it."

"What will?"

"They need help. A family member, a friend or a counsellor to sit on the seat next to them and guide them. A person who can motivate or ask them where they are going. Someone who can help them off this roundabout."

We travelled for over an hour. Tens of thousands of buses followed around, going nowhere. Every few hundred yards our bus would move into another lane, drawing closer to the centre. I felt drowsy watching the almost slow-motion scene play out before me.

"I like it here," I admitted. "Everything has such a slow rhythm. We're one amongst a river of buses. It feels comforting. Let's stay on and go around again."

"You're getting sucked in. Our exit ramp is only a few hundred yards away. Decide to leave. If you don't, you could find yourself stuck here."

"Once more, Grandad, please."

Grandad gave in and followed the other buses. We drifted even closer to the centre.

"I'm finding it hard to keep control, Jack."

I knew what Grandad meant. I wanted to close my eyes and drift off. Most of the buses didn't have drivers. Many of them sat further back on their buses, not interested in which direction their vehicle was heading. Some didn't even look up; instead their eyes were focused squarely on their TV or tablets, watching anything that would distract them from the road ahead.

"Grandad. No one is driving these buses. They are engrossed online or watching box sets."

"Exactly what I expected. They get sucked into the land of nothingness. People keeping themselves distracted, anything rather than facing up to the world. It makes life easier for them if they forget about themselves, their partner or children. They distract themselves instead of talking to or enjoying activities with their friends and family."

"Do you really think that's how it is?"

"I'm positive. Another thing, have you noticed this round-about is growing extra lanes with every mile we're travelling? Very few are taking the decision to leave. But the number of people joining is growing."

I glanced across the lanes of traffic, feeling pleased a few buses had left by the exits. However, more buses swerved on from the slip roads, the roundabout expanding from the flow of new buses. The traffic on the middle island wasn't moving. It was at a standstill.

"What's happening in the centre, Grandad?"

"Broken-down buses. Look at them. Wheels missing, bonnets up, hammocks stretched between the vehicles – these drivers have given up completely. They're not moving. They're waiting for others to take care of them."

"Can't we help them?"

"We can try," said Grandad. He leant out the window and waved to the people sitting in the centre. "Do you need any help?"

Most ignored us. A few responded, laughing. One man shouted back. "Help with what? We're managing fine without you. Leave us alone."

I climbed down onto the step and opened the door. "Follow us, we'll take you out of here."

"Go away," a woman said. "Leave us in peace."

A man sitting on a deckchair called to us. "Park your bus and join us. Stop rushing around. You can stay as long as you want. We have a good life."

Grandad looked at me. "This is what no direction or ambition does to people. They rarely follow anyone. They'll lose everything in their life by not trying."

"But why don't they take our help and improve their lives? We can help them get away from here."

"It's pointless. They're settled. If they came with us, they would have to make a lot of hard decisions. They may not be ready for that. Now, Jack, we need to get off ourselves before we get sucked in and stuck forever. I have to navigate through this traffic to get back to the outside and it's tight with no space to manoeuvre. The buses are so crammed in I'll never get through."

"Can I help, Grandad?"

"Make a decision. A positive one."

"I've decided I want to go to the Best Seat in the Universe, now!"

The words had hardly left my mouth when the traffic opened up in the lane beside us. Grandad eased through, taking us away from the centre. We were now beyond the slowest moving buses. I repeated my decision a few times until we reached the outer lanes. A few drivers tried to block us but were unsuccessful.

One shouted at us. "What's your hurry? Where are you going?"

Grandad opened his window and shouted back. "We're going somewhere. That's all you need to know."

The man shrugged his shoulders. "Somewhere? Who wants to go there?"

"It's better than nowhere," Grandad replied. He eased his bus into the outer circle. There were so few buses leaving the roundabout. He saw his exit and headed towards it, joining a major road.

"I was getting lazy, Grandad. I could have stayed and snuggled into one of those hammocks with a blanket."

"It's an easy trap, son. That's why a plan is important."

"Why don't they do what we did and decide?"

"They live in a world of fear."

"Fear of what?"

"Simple things. Taking control, being a breadwinner, people laughing at them."

"Surely there's nothing difficult in that?"

"Correct. But fear is unjustified. It makes most situations seem far worse than they are."

"I don't understand what they are frightened of."

"Failure. Looking stupid in front of others. Fear of themselves, fear of the unknown. Imposter syndrome and lack of self-belief are the biggest issues. It stems from false messages given to them during childhood."

"I don't understand. What could people say to make them frightened as adults?"

"Since childhood, they've been told they won't amount to much. It ruins their self-confidence. They believe they'll never fit in, never be good enough. Little by little, they believe it. When they go for a job interview, these negative words haunt them. They get frightened, lose confidence and avoid applying for employment. It becomes a self-fulfilled prophecy. If they don't get a job, they believe those who told them they were no good were right. They convince themselves they aren't good enough. They appear like an outcast and these wrong beliefs turn to reality."

"Can we go back and help them, Grandad?"

"We can't, Jack, we're running out of time and I have to get you back. Let's leave it to their families or the professionals, the many carers who work hard in the community to help these poor souls to feel pride in themselves. It's not a one-day fix. It takes time and commitment to help people back towards a meaningful life: believing in them, complimenting them and helping them gain confidence."

The roundabout haunted me. I couldn't understand why so

many people had become stuck, going nowhere in life. It all felt so sad.

I sighed. "Where to next, Grandad?"

"I'm going to show you how others can influence you and how to make sure you trust in your decisions."

"Sounds good. Let's go."

Grandad set a new destination:

BE FAITHFUL TO YOURSELF

TEN

BE FAITHFUL TO YOURSELF

We were enjoying our adventure. It felt like we'd stolen a bus and ran away. We'd always been close, but this was different. I didn't want it to end.

A woman standing at the side of the road waved us down. Grandad stopped and let her climb aboard. She asked him not to drive off, as she'd only be a minute. She handed me a brightly coloured leaflet and asked how I came to be here. I told her about our arrival.

She nodded and a strange look passed over her eyes. "Go back beyond the veil," she said. She waved as she stepped from the bus.

"What did she want?" Grandad asked.

I looked at her leaflet. "It says *Be Faithful*. I suppose that's a good thing."

"It sure is, son. But the question is, to whom should you be faithful? Society says: be faithful to your wife, your partner, your family, your community. I'm not so sure it's that easy."

"Really? Surely it's a simple thing to do?"

"Is it? It takes a lot of effort and self-control to lead a life pleasing others."

"But it's worth the effort, don't you think, if you make other people happy?"

"Perhaps. My issue is if you work at keeping others satisfied, then it means you risk not being faithful to yourself. I'd rather be faithful to myself first, before everyone else."

"Can't you be faithful to everyone?"

"No, Jack, that's not possible. People have so many demands and viewpoints of life, things that you would never agree with. Respect their views by all means, but don't waste your life trying to please them."

"What do you think the leaflet should say?"

"I would rather it read *Be faithful to yourself, your life and your beliefs and, where possible, to others*."

"Isn't that the same thing?"

"No. Being faithful to yourself allows you to follow your heart and your dreams. Anything less means you are failing the gift this life has given you. Trying to please others, including family members, can restrict you and create difficult decisions. Things you may believe in, they may not."

"In what way?"

"Jack, what goes on in each person's head is principally a solo journey. Every person decides what they love and what they want to be in this world. When you try to please others, they may prefer you to do things differently. They might try to convince you to do things their way."

Grandad was making sense. I knew I did things to please others, which wasn't what I always wanted to do.

"This is your life, son. Only you can live it. It's your world. Surround yourself with good people. Have real aims. But first and foremost, make sure you are faithful to your own aims and dreams. If you reach the end of your life and know you achieved every ambition you chased, then it's mission accomplished. Make sound decisions and stick by them."

"Isn't it selfish to be faithful only to myself?"

"Not at all. I'm not saying don't help others. I'm suggesting you should work with them if it fits in with your life. Don't be swayed by another person's dreams; be true to your own. If you live life following what others suggest would be good for you, you compromise yourself and are on the wrong path. Living to another person's rules ruins so many people's lives. As soon as others dictate to you, you are not in control or living life the way you should."

"That's what I want, Grandad, to live my own life."

"Great. If everyone could stop and think for a few minutes and promise to be faithful to themselves, the world would be a far happier place. When you compromise to please others, it satisfies no one. That route creates conflict within yourself. Once conflict arises, unhappiness creeps in. Your unhappiness leads to bitterness from not doing what you truly want, and this means you are not being faithful to yourself."

"I still think some people would see it as selfish..."

"It may look that way to others, but it's not. If you are doing what you want, you will be happy. If you are happy, the people you surround yourself with will feed off your positive energy and be happy too. If your life is not happy, you've compromised to please others. You get pushed and pulled in all directions. You can't concentrate on what is good for you because compromising has made you unhappy."

"I understand."

"When you live the way you want, it will settle you. The people you try to please will make you angry by the power they try to exert over you. It's back to what I was saying about driving your own bus. If you are in control, you can do so much more. If you can do much more with a clear head, you can help more people, but it will be on your terms, not theirs. It's important to be faithful to yourself first and reliable to others second."

"I get it. It helps when you spell it out for me."

"Let's move on, Jack. We've still a long way to go."

"Where to next Grandad?"

"We're going to look at how you are influenced by others."

I read the board:

CIRCLES OF INFLUENCE

ELEVEN

CIRCLES OF INFLUENCE

W e wound through the narrow streets of an old village lined with Tudor-style buildings. The white walls and dark wooden beams made strange patterns. I remembered seeing this architecture in a documentary about England.

Grandad's bus struggled up and down the minor roads, the gears crunching as he manhandled the small twists and turns. A trail of exhaust plumed behind us with every push on the accelerator.

"This is the life, son, touring through these traditional villages. You never know what you'll see in a place like this."

"I know, it goes from one extreme to the other. The buildings in the village are ancient. It's like stepping back in time."

"If you think this is wild, wait until you find the Best Seat in the Universe. That will be the experience of a lifetime."

"What does it look like, Grandad?"

He didn't answer. He was concentrating, squeezing around some tight corners. We drove on in silence for a while before he spoke again.

"Jack, you're not listening to me, you're daydreaming. You need to keep alert."

"I'm not, Grandad, I was trying to imagine what we would see when we arrive."

"Don't waste time imagining. Wait until you get there."

He was right. No point in trying to think of what anything would look like in this strange world.

"Sorry, son. I'm trying to influence you by suggesting you find the Best Seat in the Universe, but I shouldn't do that. Doing so means I'm no better than the circles of influence who have been filling your head since you were born."

"The what?"

"Circles of influence. You know who I mean: friends, family, teachers, in fact almost everyone you've ever come into contact with and who has had a say in your life or at least tried to."

"I lead my own life, Grandad. No one tells me what to do except Mum and Dad, and the odd comment from you, of course." I winked at him.

He shook his head. "That's not true, Jack. We are all controlled to a point by those around us. Parents tell children how to think based on their experiences. They suggest you become a doctor, politician, or maybe part of the family business."

"That's true. Mum wants me to work on the farm. To be honest, I can't think what else I would do. I only know farming."

"Wouldn't it be so much better if she asked you, at least gave you a choice of what you want to do?"

"I suppose."

"When you are sitting at the big tree with your friends, they also try to influence you. They tell you to ignore what your parents say and to do what they're doing. In school, it's the teachers telling you what you could be. Outstanding teachers influence you by reinforcing your dream and your positive attitude. Unfortunately, poor teachers put fear in your head of how you will fail, never get a good job and end up on the scrapheap. All these people influence you."

"Does it matter that much?"

"It does. You will carry some of those thoughts for a lifetime and if they are good, that's brilliant, but what about when they are negative?"

"I never thought of that."

"Tell me, Jack, what are your thoughts on the travelling community?"

"Good people, why?"

"You're saying that because I influenced you. When I was young, my parents told me the travelling community were not trustworthy. They said they would steal our crops and machinery. I regarded them as criminals my entire life and chased them away for a long time."

"What changed?"

"I was in my forties when one day I broke down at the side of the road. Two travellers stopped and helped me, and they wouldn't take any kind of payment. They only wanted to help. I questioned my beliefs on what I'd been told about this community. I worked closer with them and it was a positive thing for me and the farm. For over thirty years I lived with that nonsense in my head, fed to me from my parents and other farmers. Their fears were leading me. How stupid was that?"

"I wonder why they told you not to trust them?"

"Therein lies the issue. When you trust in those close to you, you have no reason to doubt them. Maybe at some point they had something to complain about, but because one person may take advantage of you doesn't mean to say you can make the assumption that everyone from that community is the same. This is what people do. They spread their fears or prejudices, which can affect you for years. The travellers are fine with me, and many remain good friends. They have helped me fix machinery, bring in crops and lay traps to stop mice eating all the grain. Sometimes you get a couple of scallywags, but that's no different from many others in the farming community. If I had questioned my beliefs earlier, my unfounded suspicions would have disappeared many years ago."

"I hear what you are saying. Things I've been told may not be as true as they seem."

"That's exactly it, Jack. Because we trust our friends and family, we have no reason to doubt anything they tell us."

"That makes sense and yet it doesn't."

"I agree. But it's not only them. We're influenced by people who lived thousands of years ago, which sounds crazy, but it's true. They have brainwashed us into thinking if advice is old, then it must be true."

"But surely it makes sense if they have passed it down through the generations? There must be some truth in it."

Grandad sighed. "Sometimes, but not always. Many good things last the test of time because they seem right in every way. Other times, ancient guidance can be terrible. Worse, though, we aren't allowed to question these ways for fear of punishment."

"Why wouldn't we question them?"

"That's the attitude. The threat of punishment scares people to question everything. So, they live their lives influenced by people who lived thousands of years ago. The world has moved on and should rethink influence from any period other than the present."

"Is this about religion, Grandad?"

"Not in particular. For example, there are many influential texts, whether religious or otherwise."

"Someone must think they were worthwhile keeping."

"You're correct, but Einstein was a genius and Aristotle a great philosopher. It doesn't mean that everything they ever uttered is relevant. Remember, our ancestors would also have had a sense of humour, so who knows which parts may have been a joke." There was a twinkle in his eye.

"That would be funny, Grandad, if we were all bowing down to something that was meant to be a joke."

Grandad laughed. "I'm sure it has happened. Learn to question everything, son. It doesn't matter how old a rule is or who wrote it. Remember, I wasted thirty years fearing the travelling community through poor information. What do you think has been put in my head in the name of religion? Don't let anyone pass their fears on to you."

"Why would I question what I'm told is true?"

"Because things can only be true when you agree to it."

"That makes no sense." This was getting confusing. "If it's true, it's true."

"Well, one person's truth is not always the same as another's. People have different beliefs. We have different thoughts on what is good and evil, right and wrong. We also have different levels of tolerance of these things."

"I get it, Grandad. It's incredible how complex people are."

"That's true. People try to persuade communities with their versions of truth or fear."

"Why?"

"Usually, power or money, sometimes both."

"So, who can we trust?"

"Yourself, Jack. You are the only thing you control. Trust what you do. Also, trust what you feel in your heart. Your heart is rarely wrong. Whatever situation you are in, ask yourself, does this feel right? Remain as innocent as you can. Ask simple questions, and these should be answerable with simple answers. When an answer becomes complex, be alert. Most things are straightforward. They only get complicated when people twist and turn and try to deceive. Question advice from others like you would question yourself. Watch out for the strangest answer of them all: 'Do as I say and not as I do.' When you hear these words, Jack, you are witnessing an advice giver who can't follow their own advice. It's one of the biggest cop-outs you'll ever hear."

"I understand, Grandad."

"Carve a path made from your beliefs. That's why we have free will. Once you decide to live from the heart and trust it, you will live an honest life."

I fell silent for a moment, as I gazed out at the darkness. "Grandad, how come you've never shared these ideas with me before?" I said at last.

"I made the mistake of allowing the wrong people to limit my development. No one advised me to question things. If anything, the opposite is true. Never question an adult, they would say, as if adults have all the answers. Teachers, doctors and scout leaders, they all knew better than me, and it was rude as a teenager to question them. But you have the advantage. You can take control of your life far earlier than I did. I took a long time to work it out. As soon as I did, however, I was free. I still find it hard to understand why I was so easily misguided."

"Maybe because your parents accepted what they learned and questioned nothing."

"That's true and a big part of it. My life completely changed the night I met a couple camping at the big tree. I joined them for a coffee, and we talked all night. It turned out to be the most important night of my life."

"That's a bold statement, Grandad."

"I know, but it's true. We had a night full of discussion, which gave me a perspective into life I had never questioned. They told me about the world, philosophy, freedom, following one's heart and so many things. And I loved it most when they talked about truth. My life changed there and then. I had so many questions and I needed answers. It took me years of unlearning before I worked out what my life was about. Other people's thoughts placed inside my head since childhood had done so much damage."

"How can you unlearn what you've been told, Grandad?"

He glanced over and gave me a sympathetic look. "It's actually very hard. You have to question everything and reassess everything you think you know or have been told. To become innocent again, open, trusting and curious meant I had to revisit and question everything. Everyone is influenced and corrupted by others and their ways. Try not to pass your thoughts on to others as if they are gospel. It's the corruption of man. It would be better if people told you what they did in a certain situation and then ask you how you would approach a similar thing. At least then you would have the chance to learn your own way."

"I get it, Grandad."

"Resist taking advice from people who don't have any faith in you to think for yourself."

"But I can't ignore members of my own family, can I?"

"No, don't stop talking to them. But recognise those who are not helping you achieve your dream. If they give you advice, take it on board if it's good and let it go if it's useless. Be friendly either way."

"I will, Grandad." I smiled and shook my head. "The problem is, now I'm not sure what you are telling me is the best thing for me."

Grandad's eyes lit up. "Excellent, Jack! Understand what I'm saying. I'm not telling you how to think; I'm giving you a method to help you make choices for yourself. It's your decision whether you want this. So, let me ask you, do you still want to go to The Best Seat in the Universe?"

"My heart is saying I should, Grandad."

"Good. That's all you ever need. Let's go and see how your life can be redirected in the briefest moment."

He spun the handles again:

BRIEF ENCOUNTER

TWELVE

BRIEF ENCOUNTER

G randad was talkative. His voice was pitching up and down, and his enthusiasm was infectious. We passed several places when I noticed a symbol I'd seen before and remembered Grandad had one on his keyring.

"Grandad, what does that symbol mean?"

"It's an ancient Chinese sign: the yin and yang. One of the oldest and most powerful ever created. It's very significant. If you understand the meaning of this, you understand the balance of life itself. I wish I'd discovered it far earlier; it would have made life clearer to me."

"In what way?"

"I would have had a better understanding of this world and a more balanced view."

I couldn't imagine how a simple symbol could make such a difference. "Where did you discover the meaning?" I asked.

"It's an unusual story." Grandad stared at the road ahead. "I've never shared it before, because it's very personal. I tried to tell your grandma, but she wouldn't listen. She said it was a load of hocus-pocus. I learnt to keep quiet about it and never told your mother. It's only now I can speak to you about it."

I was intrigued. "Tell me."

"Okay. The night I discovered the meaning of the yin and yang symbol was an awakening for me that changed my entire outlook on life. I realised how I'd walked the wrong path for a large part of my life. This realisation brought me comfort, power and wisdom all at once. I changed how I viewed every situation." His eyes met mine briefly. "It happened because grandma and I had a flaming row."

"You argued with Grandma? I don't believe it." Grandma and Grandad had always seemed like they had the easiest, happiest relationship.

"We didn't row often. But this time we did, and it was ugly. Like most arguments, it was silly. I wanted to go abroad, leave American shores and visit Europe. Your grandma was totally against it because she didn't like travel. She did everything in her power to stop me. She cried and screamed and accused me of abandoning her, which, of course, I would never do. I wanted her to come and travel with me, but she didn't want to."

"Why not?"

"She was frightened of visiting other countries. It was as simple as that."

"I'm so surprised," I admitted.

"It's the way she was. Mostly a loving woman, and I loved her unbelievably so, but I had regrets and felt restricted from doing the things I wanted."

I would never have guessed. "It sounds dreadful. So you argued?"

"We did, and it lasted for hours. It was after midnight when I stormed out of the house. I'm now sure some things happen for a reason and this was one of those times my life changed radically."

"What could happen at midnight that could create such a major change?"

"Let me explain. It was dark when I left the house. I headed across the fields, not knowing where I was going. Upset, I tried to work out why we'd argued so much. The moon was bright and shone across the top of the swaying crops. Thoughts of leaving your grandma to start a new life filled my head. But your mother was only a young girl, and I loved nothing more than to spend time with her. I couldn't consider leaving. I was happiest when I tucked her up safely in bed every night. I couldn't live without being in the company of your mum every day, so I had to solve our problem."

"Couldn't you have seen her at weekends?" I asked, thinking of my friend whose parents were divorced.

"No, Jack, I couldn't. I treasured every moment of your mum growing up. I would have gone crazy if it had separated us. Even now we see each other most days. She's ... she's everything to me."

"We love seeing you every day too," I said, without thinking. "It makes our day complete."

Grandad stopped and let out a long, shaky breath. He

wiped the tears from the corner of his eyes with the back of his hand. "Where was I?"

"You were walking through the fields at midnight."

"So I was. I walked a fair distance, not sure where I was heading. Field after field I crossed, before heading to the big tree to gather my thoughts."

"You went to my tree?"

"Jack, what you and your friends do today, we did fifty years ago. We had our pow-wows there. Every one of us sat with our girlfriends and swam in the river. My father did the same thirty years earlier. You and your friends are not the first to make the big tree your meeting place and you won't be the last. If you stay at the farm, your children and grandchildren will probably do the same."

I smiled. It was strange to think Grandad had hung out at my tree all those years ago.

"I didn't want to waken any of my friends. To tell you the truth, I felt embarrassed and didn't want anyone to know your grandma and I had argued. I climbed the tree and settled down into the crook of the branches and sat there, thinking. I must have dozed off and wakened when I heard singing. I thought I was dreaming. One o'clock in the morning and out of the darkness, voices laughing and singing. I climbed down and made my way towards them."

"Were they poachers?"

"No. They were loud. Poachers wouldn't make a sound. I crept closer and spotted their campfire. A couple sat there, singing their hearts out. As I came out of the shadows, I startled them. They froze. The woman jumped up and backed towards the man. She said I was to take what I wanted and leave."

"Why did she say that?"

"She must have thought I was a thief. The man stood beside the fire holding his guitar. It was tense for a minute before their kettle started to whistle. 'Is there enough coffee in your pot for one more?' I asked them. 'Sure,' the man said. But they still looked uncomfortable.

"The woman cleared her throat and asked if I was travelling through. I told them that I lived there, and she asked me if they were trespassing on my land. 'I promise we won't make a mess,' she said. I told her not to worry and explained why I was out during the night. After that, they relaxed and we drank our coffee. They told me their names were Bob and Joan, and they were touring the area in their VW camper van. They were a hippie couple from England, travelling across America on a journey of self-discovery."

"Excellent. I'd love to take a closer look at my own life."

"It's funny you say that, Jack, because back then I didn't understand what self-discovery meant when they mentioned that phrase. What they told me blew my mind."

"Sounds crazy."

"It sure was. They answered questions I'd thought about before I ever met them. Big life questions of which I never knew how to find the answers. Every word they spoke switched on lightbulbs in my head. They were affirming thoughts I'd had for years. No one in my circle of friends was thinking this way. It was a night of wonder. We sang songs and traded stories. I was full of admiration for the way they lived. They'd visited so many countries. I'd only ever left my hometown to attend the agricultural shows in the next state. I felt ashamed that I'd never really been anywhere outside my own country. Like most others from this area, I'd been told America had everything and so there was no reason to go abroad. Bob and Joan told me otherwise, with stories of different cultures, warm people and a lifetime of memories. This is what I wanted to experience. And it was the exact reason I'd fallen out with your grandmother earlier that evening."

"These people were enjoying a life of freedom."

"They were. Everywhere they travelled, they explored spiritually. For five years they lived with other cultures. They were seeking an inner way through encounters with both land and people."

"Sounds a bit out there."

"It was, Jack, but it was beautiful. I'd never heard of anyone searching for enlightenment. I took on board everything they told me. I'd been seeking this for years without knowing what it was. Here it was, laid out bare in front of me. One brief encounter with two wonderful souls and my head was bursting. They suggested books to read. Words from gurus and eastern mystics with tales of the inner being. This was beyond my imagining. Until that night, I had only read Mark Twain and Walt Whitman. The next day I went out and bought these books, which led to many more. I treasure them to this day."

"Will I be able to read them?"

"One day, Jack, one day."

"So ... what about Grandma? She must have been worried. What time did you get home?"

"Around eight in the morning. Sunrise was at six, and it was a beautiful, crisp morning. The fragrance from the flowers was rolling into our camp. Songbirds were on the wing, finding food for their young. I never laughed so much as I did in that one night. We talked until dawn. Their camper van sat beside us decorated with flowers and Peace and Love written all over it just like mine. Theirs had the sun, moon and stars painted on each side and on the back, several symbols and a joke of sorts: *Keep off the grass.* I'm sure it wasn't talking about not stepping on turf – the English have a wonderful sense of humour."

As I listened, I was reflecting on how Grandad always fitted in with whomever he met. He wasn't frightened to sit with strangers and get to know them. "You still hadn't left them to get home?"

"I was trying my best. I was shaking hands with them and saying goodbye when I saw this symbol painted on the back of their van. I'd seen it before, but was never sure what it was. So I asked Bob.

"I'll never forget his face. He smiled at me and said something like, 'You sit with us all night and ask the most important question as you are leaving.' He sat me down again next to the fire, put on another pot of fresh coffee, while Joan went to find some bread to make toast. We talked for another couple of hours. Bob explained everything he knew about this beautiful symbol to me – the yin and yang. I was awestruck. His explanation was crucial in that moment of my life. I was happy, sad, emotional and heartbroken all at once. How could I reach my mid-thirties, unaware of this life-changing knowledge? Was I ever so glad to ask a question? It turned that night into the most important of my life."

"Grandad, don't spin it out. What did he tell you?"

"Patience, Jack! It was a long answer and also one that might not mean the same to you as it did to me."

"Why not?"

"Well, let's say it helped me to make sense of who I was and where I was heading to. It was Bob who sent me on a path of questioning everything."

"Are you still in touch with them?" I wondered aloud.

"No, I never saw them again. Before we said our goodbyes, I took them to the big tree, and we climbed into the den. They loved our tree and said they would cherish our night together as long as they lived. They invited me to travel with them for a while. In my heart I wanted to go with them more than anything, but I couldn't leave your mother. Regretfully, I declined their offer. That night taught me one of the most important lessons in my life."

"What was it?"

"How could two people I met only briefly change my life so dramatically? What they did in one evening was more than my community had done for me in my entire life. I learnt a lesson: If you meet a person for the first time, make it memorable. You never know if the next person you meet will change your life."

"Do you regret never seeing them again?"

"I have no regrets, but I would love to meet them again and tell them how they set me on a journey of self-discovery for the next thirty-plus years. I would love to shake their hands and thank them because they helped me discover who I am inside, the real me."

Grandad fascinated me. I had never seen him as animated as he was now. I could only see happiness in his eyes as he relived that night.

"Bob told me he suspected our paths would cross again, but if they didn't, then I was to take everything from that moment that I could. 'Maybe we'll meet on this path again or maybe in the next life, whichever comes first,' he said, and put his arms around me and held me for a long time. It was the first time another man had hugged me, and it didn't seem odd. It felt natural because of the way they lived. They both had this distinctive fragrance, which I loved. Bob told me he rubbed Patchouli extract on his arms. To this day, every time I smell that scent, Bob and Joan come rushing into my head. It made me aware of how something as simple as a scent can bring back so many memories."

I smiled. "That's a wonderful story. I wish I'd met them. Tell me about the yin and yang."

"I will, Jack, after I finish what happened that morning. I walked home with a spring in my step. I felt rejuvenated, overflowing with an energy through my body that I'd never felt before. I knew from that day forward I would change my outlook and the way I lived."

"Did you, Grandad?"

"I did, but it took time. "When I arrived home, I was so excited to tell your grandma about Bob and Joan. Unfortunately, all I faced was a torrent of anger. She called me every name under the sun. It wasn't pretty. She'd thought I'd stayed with another woman. She accused me of having an affair, which wasn't true. She burst my bubble and I felt deflated. It set me back for a while. I had to figure out how to get my life back on track. I had lots of thinking time when working the fields. I bought the books Bob suggested. I cried many times, reading the wisdom between those pages. This led me to more books, and now I have quite a collection. The books all had one thing in common, and that was to help a seeker look inwards and question who they are."

"Did Grandma read the books?"

"No. Don't be silly. She thought it was all airy fairy rubbish. Gobbledegook, she called it. She said I was mad thinking a book could change my life. But she was wrong. I had changed, and it was not only from reading those books. My life changed the moment I sat around the campfire with Bob and Joan."

"Why wouldn't she listen?"

"Fear. Fear of the unknown, fear of a different way of thinking. Nothing but plain fear and ignorance."

"Didn't she want to learn what you were reading?"

"No. She believed we shouldn't question what our parents taught us. Small-minded thinking. Unfortunately, she didn't want to explore other possibilities and so I never pushed it, as I believe in each to their own in matters like this."

"Didn't it annoy you? You had found this wonderful thing, these new beliefs, and yet you couldn't share them."

"It didn't matter. The important thing was that my world had changed. I had changed. While your grandma rejected any alternative ways of thinking, I understood her and knew in my heart I couldn't change her. When we argued, it didn't matter. I could go deep within my head and stay calm and be at peace. I developed techniques to help my life and sanity and moved on. I could still live with your grandma and be happy. It was only certain times like her not wanting to travel or leave our farm that caused me pain."

"I'm sorry about Grandma not understanding ... but what about the yin and yang symbol?" I persisted. "What was so special about it?"

"Let's stop and get a drink and I'll tell you."

Grandad pulled into a roadside café.

THIRTEEN

BALANCE OF LIFE

W e left our bus and headed into a diner. It was a traditional 1950s truck stop, decorated in black, white and red. Bar stools ran the length of the old counter, while the floor and walls were decorated with chequered tiles. Grandad was still grinning, thinking of his adventure with Bob and Joan. The waitress filled our cups and served us breakfast. Her hand rested on her hip while her mouth fought hard with a large piece of gum. She blew bubbles and stared at us.

"You guys ain't the type we normally serve. Where did you drift in from?"

I didn't know where to look. I tried to see why she thought we were different, but we didn't look out of place with the regulars.

"We're from beyond the veil," said Grandad.

"Is that right?" She frowned. "Can I get you anything else?"

Grandad nodded. "Can I borrow your notepad and pen?"

Her eyes narrowed. "I rarely get that type of request. Are you two educated or something?" She ripped a few pages from her notebook and picked one of three pens she had in her top pocket. "Will this do?"

Grandad smiled. "Perfect."

"And I'll be hoping for a tip when you pay your check."

Grandad gave her the thumbs up. He placed the ketchup bottle on top of the paper and traced a circle around the bottom. He drew a wavy line from one end of the circle to the other. On each half of the circle, he drew two small circles. He coloured one in black and left the napkins natural colour for the white half. He finished by shading a small circle of black. He showed me his handiwork, pleased with his effort.

"This is the yin and yang," he said, presenting his drawing. "The Chinese created this symbol to explain the concept of dualism hundreds, if not thousands, of years ago. This was painted on the outside of Bob and Joan's camper van and is also what you see on my bus."

I NODDED IN RECOGNITION.

"Sitting at the campfire, Bob explained the meaning behind

this symbol. I would say he gave me a formula for understanding life. From that day forward I looked at everything differently, and I've been guided by it ever since. He told me it's all about balance."

"How can balance teach you about life? I think Bob put something in your tea that night."

Grandad laughed. "Maybe you're right." He winked at me. "You know how we often see white as good and black as evil? The good guys wear white and the bad guys wear black. You know that, don't you?"

"Sure."

"So, this yin and yang is half black and half white: opposites linked by their duality. Day and night are both different, but each merge into the other. Each depends on the other to exist. The cleverness of this symbol is the two small dots. This shows us for both sides to be balanced perfectly, they each have to contain an element from their opposite."

"I think I understand."

"Good. Whatever is happening to you in life, try to see this symbol and understand that the opposite part will also be there. Even if you can't see it at that moment, trust that it will be there."

"Can you give me an example?"

"Of course. Everything good that happens to you will have part of the opposite within it. That's what the small dot represents. So, if you have success in business, within that somewhere you will have failure. Maybe you've made money, but you've treated your staff poorly or not given the customer the service they paid for."

"Is this only about good and bad, then?"

"No, Jack, it's about opposites and the duality of all forces. You can't have one without the other. Within every bit of failure, you learn something new and that learning is an incremental success step for you. The failure is the black half and the white dot is the success learning step."

"I see."

"What you know from this symbol is they have to exist to balance each other. Right and wrong, rich and poor, man and woman, love and hate, day and night, land and water, success and failure. Wherever one thing exists its opposite is also present. When you recognise this, everything makes sense and life becomes easier to understand."

"You said love and hate. Are you telling me within love there's a small part which is hate?"

"That's it. A couple fall in love and life is perfect. And then the small things happen. The toothpaste lid is left off, the toilet seat is standing up, or a room is a mess. One of them may become upset by this, and these small things become magnified. Every bathroom visit they see the toothpaste lid and the toilet seat and they get angry ... but they are also in love, so they don't want to upset their new partner."

"Doesn't sound like it's worth the argument."

"I agree, but it's a part of the balance, the yin and yang, so it has to be there. One day it becomes too much and the shouting starts. Tempers flare, and it all spills out. The small dot of hatred has come to the fore. The argument ensues and for the first time this loving couple are now at odds. It becomes bitter and they scream and shout, and the hatred side of the yin and yang is now dominant. After a while, they calm down. They talk it through and make up. The small dot of love in the hatred side grows. They apologise to each other and the dot grows bigger and they become closer and will remain balanced until one part forces the next fallout."

I took a moment to digest this, imagining it visually. "Wow, Grandad, I could almost picture it happening in the symbol as you explained it. I never knew we could see this in a simple design."

"Well, it's useful to understand, so you foresee these things and know opposites exist. You may be rich or poor, happy or sad, married or single, home bird or traveller – the sign will guide you."

"I think I'll practice with it to get a better understanding."

"I agree. It took me years. I recall realising that not every rich person is fortunate, because they often suffer poverty in a way we don't."

"How can the rich suffer poverty?"

"A rich person can't buy family, love or friends, and these are all areas that make life worth living. If they have no one to share their good fortune with, they can be miserable. They accept that money only makes them happy to a low level. It becomes a burden. The people who surround them may only be there because they spend money on them. If their wealth disappeared tomorrow, would these so-called 'friends' also go? In that way, their poverty may be demonstrated in friendship. I would rather have friends than money, Jack."

"Me too, although a few extra dollars wouldn't do us any harm." I smiled.

"True." Grandad chuckled and took a sip of his coffee. "Imagine the ocean, thousands of square miles of water, and in the middle sits a tiny island. Sailors love the expanse and challenges of the sea and yet there is no drinkable water, and so this island becomes their focus. It's more important than the ocean itself. And the opposite is true of the caravans that cross thousands of miles of hot, dry deserts where few things can survive the torturous heat. The travellers understand the value of a tiny watering hole against the vastness of the desert."

"So good men have a dark side to them?"

"Correct. Even saints have sin within them, and sinners

have compassion within them. It has to be. Watch a criminal with his children. He can't help but give them love."

"So how do I use this symbol to guide me?"

"Easy. Understand you hold the potential of many things within you. Recognise the opposite will always be there and try to plan how you would deal with it. Better to look at it in advance than to wait until you can't handle a developing problem."

"I think I understand."

"Jack, some people start their own business with the aim of changing their lifestyle. They want to work fewer hours than their employer forces them to work now. They want a bigger wage so they can have more treats for their family. It's all on the white side. That's why I say look at it in advance. What if their new business doesn't bring them higher earnings? What if they have to work double the hours? What if...? That's why if you look at the balance beforehand, you can plan appropriately. I don't know many businesses where the owner hasn't worked more hours for less money in the first couple of years. That dream lifestyle is often attainable, but it takes time. Understand the opposite is there so you can accept it in advance. Once you can do this, negative developments rarely bother you."

"How do you accept it in advance?"

"Bob believed in peace and love. But others out there want war. He wanted love, they wanted hate. Bob didn't hate, but he tired of the politicians creating wars and seeing young soldiers dying for no good reason. He hated the politicians, which was not his way. He recognised this was the duality within him and knew from the yin and yang it had to be there. His hatred seemed worse to him, because he was a man of peace."

"Wasn't he right to hate the politicians, especially if he saw people were being killed?"

"More hate never improves the situation. Instead he chose

to change other people's way of thinking. A slow and frustrating path, perhaps, but a better path."

"It seems simple and yet complex at the same time."

"It is. The travelling community wishes for a piece of land to settle down and the city dwellers want to travel and have freedom. Opposites exist everywhere. Recognising them gives us a better understanding of the whole."

Things were beginning to make sense. I began to feel an awakening within me, and told Grandad so.

"That's wonderful, Jack. So many people walk around asleep to life and miss so much. Embrace this symbol and it will help you look for the parts that give you a greater understanding. Everything has an opposite, and it's needed to be part of the whole. It wouldn't be whole without it."

"It sounds like everyone would benefit if they could understand the yin and yang symbol."

"Absolutely. Think of the opposites of ordinary and greatness. Within every person, we imagine there is only the ordinary, the humdrum activities of life where nothing happens. But that small dot of greatness is there too, and it needs to show itself now and again. Taking that small hidden dot and releasing it can help some people transform from ordinary to extraordinary."

"I'm loving the yin and yang already, Grandad."

"Excellent, Jack. All I know is once people understand it, it brings balance and greater harmony in understanding all that is around them."

I realised with a start that the waitress had been standing before us, looking at the symbol. "So, are you saying that on one side there is me in my humdrum job, but if I search within, I could do my singing and become great?" she said, popping her gum.

"We all have the tools within us to be great at something,"

Grandad replied. "All you have to do is find yours and follow your dream."

We left a pile of coins on the table and headed towards Grandad's bus, painted with flowers, peace signs and the yin and yang emblazoned across the side.

"Hey, what kind of money is this?" shouted the waitress after us.

Grandad smiled. "Let's go."

We walked back to the bus, and I was feeling a little light-headed. "Didn't you think the waitress was a bit strange, Grandad?"

"What do you mean?"

"The way she stared at us. I just thought she was wasn't normal, like us."

Grandad's eyes pierced into me. He reached his arm around my shoulder. "We're all made to be different, Jack. None of us is the same nor should we try to be. I think we need to add in another destination, a place that helps us to understand differences."

He spun the handles towards a new destination:

JUDGE YE NOT

FOURTEEN

JUDGE YE NOT

Grandad drove his bus along a beautiful four-lane avenue. On each side of the road, mature broadleaf trees stood in perfect alignment, many of them hundreds of years old. The trees were in full bloom, their leaves rippling on a gentle breeze, forty shades of green mixed with autumnal oranges and reds. It felt majestic.

He slowed down at the traffic lights. Stone buildings on each side stretched along the wide avenue. They differed from our farm buildings. I guessed they were European in design, with their tall windows, many with stained glass.

To the right of me, on a plinth, rested a bronze statue of a man dressed in eighteenth-century clothes and wearing a long, flowing cloak. He was captured in a moment of time, his right hand raised. From the statue's left hand, a long spear rose high with a flag at the top billowing in the wind, a message spelt out on its yellow background.

Judge Ye Not

I WAS STARING into the eyes of the statue when it smiled.

I rubbed my eyes. "Grandad, what does 'Judge Ye Not' mean? That way of talking sounds ancient to me and makes little sense."

"It makes perfect sense; or at least it would if people followed this rule."

"In what way?"

"It's simple. Don't make judgements about others or what they may say or do."

"Do you think that's what people do?"

"All the time. Even worse, they involve other people with their gossip. You should try to avoid this. Just like you did back there with the waitress – you said she was strange – who are you to make any form of judgement? Stick to facts, not whispers and rumours. It keeps things clear. When you judge, you are doing it from your viewpoint of the world. You don't always understand where others are or what they are going through."

I wasn't sure about this. "I think I'm an excellent judge of character."

"I thought I was too, son, until a situation many years ago unfolded in front of my eyes. It helped me not to judge so much."

"What happened?"

"I was standing at the checkout in my local store. The security guard pounced on a well-dressed man and pulled food from the lining of his coat. He had caught a thief red-handed. The people in the queue stared and some pointed at him. The woman next to me yelled he should go to prison. As we waited for the police to arrive, the line of shoppers denounced the man, saying they didn't need scum like him in their town. The man bowed his head in shame before raising it again. He looked straight at us and spoke in a soft voice and with grace. It was obvious he was well educated.

"'Please don't judge me,' he said. 'I lost my job after a serious road accident killed my wife. I have no money. My kids haven't eaten for three days, and I get no government support.'"

My eyes widened. "That's awful."

"It was, Jack. But he spoke a truth I'd never contemplated before, and it has stuck with me my entire life."

"What do you mean, a truth?"

"He said – with such clarity – 'If placed in my situation, every one of you in this queue would do as I have done to feed your children. If you wouldn't, you don't love your children. Go on and call the police and have me locked up. No one can hurt me more than I already have been hurt. No one can. The desperation I feel now is as low as any human can go. You will achieve one thing only, and that's making my kids' situation worse. The government will take them from me, and they will have lost their mother and their father.'"

"What happened?"

"Why, everyone felt terrible. The man continued, 'Perhaps you could recognise how fortunate you are and show a little humanity and let me walk away before the police arrive. I will leave these items. What crime will I have committed?'"

It was then that I noticed tears in Grandad's eyes.

"He struck me right here, Jack," he said, pointing to his heart. "He spoke the truth because if I had no money and you and your mother were hungry, I would do exactly as he did."

"Would you?"

"Without a doubt."

I had begun to feel sorry for the man. "Did he go to jail?"

"No. The woman who had been calling for his arrest paid for the items he had stolen. Some of us picked a few extra items, paid for them and added them to his basket, along with a few dollars in cash. Tears dripped from his cheeks as he bowed his head, thanking us. He left the store with more faith in humanity and with a few bags to feed his family."

"What did the police say?"

"They couldn't say anything. No crime had occurred. My fellow shoppers asked the manager to drop the charges, and he agreed and even put some extra items into the man's shopping bag himself. I'm telling you this story, Jack, because it's easy to make a snap judgement. It's easy to say right or wrong while not having all the facts. When this man was thanking us, I felt it was us who should thank him. He taught me a valuable lesson that day not to judge."

"I wonder what happened to him and his children? A few dollars wouldn't have lasted long."

"Oh, he ended up in a better position. His name was Richard. I went looking for him later that day and invited him to stay at the small cottage where my mother used to live. It was empty and made sense for his family to have a roof over their heads. They stayed a little over nine months until they got back on their feet when Richard got a job. We fed and clothed them without any expectation of payment. However, Richard was a proud man and worked hard on the farm most nights. It was a sad day and a beautiful one when they left. Sad as we had become close friends and beautiful because they'd turned their lives around and were back in control. His kids, Sam and Martha, were a breath of fresh air on the farm."

I was astounded. "You mean Uncle Sam and Aunt Martha are this man's kids?"

"Why, yes. Don't look so surprised."

"But aren't they family?" I had been convinced my favourite uncle and aunt were my blood relatives.

"They are, Jack. As close as we've got. Family doesn't always have to be through blood."

I felt shocked at Grandad's revelation. I had assumed his story was about strangers.

"Remember, their lives changed in the blink of an eye because of a car accident. Any of our lives can change in a single moment. All it takes is an accident, illness, or the simplest thing like losing your job. A change in circumstances from the normal can have a profound effect."

"It must have been hard for Uncle Sam and Aunt Martha, to lose everything like that."

"It was, and it's important to know life-changing situations happen to ordinary people every day. No one knows how they will cope until faced with adversity. So never judge another person's life. Keep an open mind and accept others as they are. Sometimes you will make snap judgements, but they should be merely a reflex until you get time to think. Step back and ask if you have all the facts. It will be a rare moment if you do."

"I'll try, Grandad." I had so much to think about.

He gave me a brisk nod. "Let's move on." He set our destination to a place that sounded as if it had so much promise:

CREATIVE PARK

Our bus zig zagged its way through the hills towards the setting sun.

FIFTEEN

ANYONE CAN BE CREATIVE

After a few hours travelling, the sky grew dark. I was getting used to this erratic behaviour with day turning to night in a very short time. We drove through a modern-looking town with glass-fronted buildings. I could see over the hedges into a nearby park. Loop after loop of fairy lights and lanterns spanned between the branches from one tree to the next, lighting up the area and giving the place a welcoming feel. Crowds gathered in circles, and in the middle, I thought I could see jugglers and other entertainers.

"Grandad, let's stop so we can visit the park." A grin stretched wide across my face. "I'd love to watch the musicians and jugglers."

"Okay, let's stretch our legs for fifteen minutes."

Grandad guided his bus towards a space near the gate of the park.

Above an archway in neon letters, the words *Creative Park* illuminated the entrance.

As soon as I stepped through the archway, I loved it. People made sculptures, instruments and toys from raw materials. I watched as artisans carved intricate designs. There were pieces of all kinds. Cats and dogs, bears, clowns, trains and a multitude of other fabulous items stood proudly at the various stalls. An elderly woman wrapped in a colourful knitted shawl waved us over.

"A gift for you," she said to me. "Price: one large smile." She held out her clasped hand and dropped a small object into my palm.

I looked down to see a tiny hand-carved mouse eating a banana. It was beautiful. I smiled even harder.

"That's it," said the woman. "I knew you had more to give."

Grandad stepped forward. "Here, let me pay for that."

"Payment was one large smile already accepted." The woman grinned. "Move along, people are standing in line."

We browsed the stalls amazed at the range of items created from wood, metal, clay, wax and paper. Artists all around were singing and performing; the entire park was alive. Grandad purchased a few artisanal candles. We went back to the bus feeling happy and sat together on the step.

"Did I ever tell you about my friends, Tom and Maisie?" he asked me.

"I don't think so."

"After your grandma passed away, sometimes Tom and Maisie would come to my home for dinner or I would go to theirs. I think they felt sorry for me living by myself, although they shouldn't have, as I've always been comfortable in my own company. They admired how I used my time well to do the things I wanted. I replied they could do the same, but they bemoaned the fact they'd wasted a lot of their life. They told me they didn't have a creative bone in their bodies. That's why they came into my head at Creative Park."

"Maybe they were telling the truth?"

"Nonsense! Everyone can create things. Here's what happened to them. We were having dinner one night when I asked Maisie if she enjoyed the meal I had cooked. 'It was wonderful,' she replied. 'Cooked to perfection as always.'

"'And what about the setting tonight?' I persisted. 'Did you enjoy having dinner by candlelight?'

"'Oh, yes,' she said, 'very cosy.' Tom nodded in agreement.

"I pointed to the candles on the table. 'Maisie, how difficult would it be to make candles like this one?' I showed her a beautiful candle sat in a decorated glass jar. She told me she didn't have a clue. I replied that it was easy and fun to do, and she retorted that she wasn't skilled at that sort of thing and had no creative flair. I looked at her. 'I made the candle you are looking at with these hands,' I said. 'I'm the least creative person in the world. I fix farm machinery. But I must tell you, it feels more special when you sit in the light of a candle you've made yourself.'

"They both stared at my candle. 'I like the different colours,' Maisie said. 'It looks fantastic.'

"'I didn't have you down as a candlemaker," Tom interrupted.

"'Ah, the beauty of life, Tom,' I replied. 'Try everything once and if you like it, try it again. If it doesn't suit, learn a different skill. Try everything while you can." He nodded. I then asked Maisie if she could bake cakes.

"'Sure,' said Maisie. 'Everyone can bake a cake.'

"'I can't. Can you teach me? I tell you what. You teach me how to bake a cake and I'll show you how to make candles.'

"'Deal.' Maisie cleared the table and showed me how to mix the flour and water and add the eggs. Before I knew it, we had baked a cake and decorated it with icing sugar. She crumbled broken walnuts on top, complementing the coffee-flavoured sponge. Then she wrote out a step-by-step set of instructions for me. I still use her recipe to this day."

I was salivating at the thought of it. "I know, Grandad. Your coffee and walnut cake is the best. Did you show Maisie how to make candles?"

"Did I show her?" Grandad's eyes lit up. "You won't believe what happened. I brought out my candle-making equipment. It doesn't comprise much more than wax, wicks of different thicknesses, a pot and different-shaped moulds. 'Maisie, you said during our meal that you and Tom dreamed of living a better life,' I said.

"'That's true,' she replied. 'Everything is so expensive. We can't seem to save much money. We make do with the small amount of savings we have.'

"'What if I showed you how to earn money creating candles? It's so simple and it may help bring in extra income."

"'We appreciate your help, but it's far too late for us,' Tom said. 'But hopefully we can pass this on to our children.'

"I told Tom to never believe it's too late. He was only sixty and still had plenty of time to achieve his goals. 'Don't let your age be a barrier,' I said.

"Tom looked at me and must have thought I was crazy. They were close to retirement and like many people of that age; they thought it was time for them to give up on what they wanted from life. Anyway, after dinner, I showed them how to melt the wax into a mould, add a wick and repeat the process. We made candles of different sizes and added colours, and when they left in the wee small hours, they were still giggling with excitement. You would've thought I had given them the secret to life. They left me that evening on a high."

I smiled at the thought. "It sounds like they had the same feeling you did when you met the people in the camper van."

"Exactly the same, Jack. A life-changing moment. When life clicks and it turns on that lightbulb in your head, it only takes that one moment, but when it comes, it's hard for your head not to be fizzing with new life. That's what happened to them."

"So what happened next?"

"I didn't see either of them for around six months. One day a formal-looking invitation arrived in my mailbox. Tom and Maisie had invited me to have dinner at their place. I was looking forward to seeing them. As I approached their house, the sun had already set. I couldn't believe what I was seeing. Their driveway resembled a beautiful runway, lit with an array of candles in glass jars of every size. I followed the lights through their front door, into their hallway and to their living room. The flickering of the flames and the fragrance was spellbinding. The scents took me back to my patchouli incense days, delighting my senses. Some candles were magnificent, standing three feet tall. I was in awe of their talent and surprised at how far they had come in such a short time.

"Maisie stepped forward and gave me a hug. 'Thank you so much,' she said. 'Look what you've done for us. You helped to change our lives in such a positive way.'

"I was amazed. I had only showed them basic candle-making, but it looked like they had made something big out of it and learned a few things I didn't know. My friends stood there grinning. The house looked like a magical scene from a fairy tale.

"Maisie squeezed my arm. 'When we left your house that evening, we agreed we hadn't had so much fun in years,' she said. 'When you told us you learnt a new hobby every year, you gave us a jolt to say life was not over. As you know, we didn't believe we had a creative bone in our bodies, but we thought maybe we could try making candles and be creative. We bought materials from the store and, after a few false starts, we learnt how to make tea lights. We were so busy and before we knew it, we had made a few hundred of these small candles. We gave many to family and friends, but we still had hundreds left. Tom was visiting our local garden centre one weekend to buy his birdseed when he noticed they had candles for sale.'

"Tom took up the story. 'It was my proudest moment,' he said. 'Without knowing why, I asked for the manager. I told him I was a candlemaker. As the words left my mouth, I was beaming and feeling a little embarrassed as I couldn't believe I said candlemaker and yet that's what we had become.'

I smiled, watching them. They looked far younger and full of life.

'I asked the manager if he would be interested in selling our tea lights,' Tom continued. 'He bought the lot and asked if we could make bigger candles. He gave us the sizes, colours and shapes he wanted. He gave me an order for fifty candles every two weeks. After six weeks our candles were so popular, he increased the order to one hundred candles every week.'

"I was amazed, but it seemed there was more to the story. 'Now we are the main candle supplier now for four gift shops and six garden centres,' Maisie announced. 'Making over six hundred candles per week. We even had to hire some help.'

"They surprised me, Jack. When I showed them how to make candles, I wanted to prove to them that everyone has a creative spark and age was no barrier. I didn't expect them to go full on towards this new business venture, but I was so glad they did. That to me personified what Bob and Joan had meant when they said that you never can tell the moment your life will change with a few words or actions from someone else. If we hadn't had the meal, Maisie and Tom would still be wandering along as before. Now they had started a business and were making more money than they'd ever dreamed of.

"They credited me for changing their lives. I hadn't, of course; I had only sown a seed. It was they who had changed. I showed them a new skill, but it was they who took action. Without action, nothing changes. I was proud of them.

"We ate our meal that night by candlelight and celebrated their success. Maisie put music on and the three of us danced *the twist*, our shadows casting over the walls from the burning candles. We were acting like teenagers again. We laughed and collapsed onto the chairs, sore with dancing and filled with joy. But Maisie had one more announcement. She fetched an envelope from her mantlepiece and asked her husband to open it. Inside was a note. He read it aloud.

To Tom, the best husband ever.
   I hope you like European food.
Love Maisie.

"Tom looked at her in surprise. He peered into the envelope and pulled out two tickets for a fourteen-day European cruise. Maisie looked like an excited schoolgirl. 'I paid for this holiday in advance,' she squealed, trying to get her words out. 'We've never been able to afford anything like this.' Tom hugged her. I was so pleased for them as Maisie breathlessly told us about all the places they would visit. They were holding onto each other and giggling. Maisie opened the window and shouted out at the top of her voice, 'I'm sixty-two years young, and for the first time in my life, I'm leaving America!'

"When I left them later that night, they gave me two presents: a beautiful watch and a large candle carved in the shape of a lighthouse. It was stunning. But the real reward for me was their success. These are the moments you can't buy, Jack. They come when you least expect them. We lived that evening in totality. Spontaneous singing and dancing, laughing with friends. There was something very special about it. It happens now and then and when it does, embrace it and step back for a moment and witness every detail you can and try to remember how special a moment you are in. Memories like these will give you a lifetime of enjoyment."

"I wish I had been there, Grandad. Tom and Maisie must be your closest friends." It was a big assumption on my part, but I had a strong feeling there was something special about this pair.

"They are, Jack. I have a good reason to tell you about Tom and Maisie. Although they were older, they found a skill set that matched their ability. They could have been successful had they started earlier, but they didn't have self-belief."

"I think there are many people like that, Grandad."

"That's true, and it's such a crime. So many creative people go unnoticed in this world. They have the talent but lack the confidence to step forward into the light. Many would love to share their skills but can't. They remain hidden in their homes and won't shout out who they are, like Maisie did from her window."

"Why don't people just go for it?" I asked.

"They fear criticism and embarrassment. People laughing at them. The saddest thing to me is to know there are people out there with incredible talents who will never gain recognition. How sad is that, Jack? All those talents crashing against the rocks."

I nodded slowly, remembering the smashed dreams at the Valley of Hope. "That's horrible, Grandad. Why would anyone laugh at creatives?"

"Fear of not understanding. Nervous that they don't get the message in their work. It's easier for them to ask the artist why they don't paint like the classics than it is for them to accept new ideas. So, when you walk down any street, Jack, know that behind those closed doors are talented people who can stand up to the best in the world. When you meet a creative person, even if you don't understand what they are doing, give them space and encouragement. Everyone has the chance to push the boundaries in their life."

I sat and thought of what Grandad had told me and wondered about my neighbours and what talents they may have.

"Jack, let's head to a place that helps to give an understanding of situations you'll likely face and how to deal with them in a balanced way."

I laughed. "That's what I love about you, Grandad. You never cease to amaze me with your insights. Where are you taking me now?"

He smiled as he turned the handles. He pointed to the board. "This one is a big deal for your peace of mind."

I read the board:

ACCEPTANCE

SIXTEEN

ACCEPTANCE OF LIFE

A loud bang shattered our thoughts. Grandad grabbed the steering wheel and fought hard to keep his bus under control. We were thrown from side to side as his bus veered wildly across the road. After a heart-stopping moment, Grandad brought his bus under control and stopped in a clearing.

We jumped off and noticed the back wheel had a missing tyre. Shreds of rubber and half a tyre lay scattered along the road.

"Unbelievable, Grandad, just what we don't need," I shouted. "We're going to miss getting to The Best Seat in the Universe. What are we going to do?"

"I'm thinking, Jack."

The panic rose up within me. "This is not good. We're stuck in the middle of nowhere. We can't call anyone to help us. What a nightmare."

"Stop fretting. It is what it is." Grandad walked around the bus. He opened the side luggage compartments and crawled in.

I wasn't comfortable, broken down in this strange place. "We're stuck and at the worst possible moment."

Grandad hauled a large metal pole from the compartment and a metal skate with steel wheels.

"You're not serious, Grandad?"

"Why not? We need to change the wheel."

"You can't raise your bus with that thing, there's no way."

"Look at the length of this lever. This will do the job." Grandad crawled back under. He struggled for breath as he tried to move the spare wheel. I crawled in beside him and pushed against the wheel with my feet. We managed to bump it onto the road.

"We didn't need this to happen, Grandad."

"Listen to yourself, son. It's a tyre that's blown and we can fix it. Stop worrying about it."

"I know, but we're—"

"Jack. When something breaks, accept it. Life happens. Get on with it."

I walked around the bus and looked at the destination board. *ACCEPTANCE*. "Grandad, the destination board says *ACCEPTANCE*. Where is this taking us?"

"Ah ... the most beautiful place. If you can learn to go there in tough times, it will help you avoid so much grief."

"But where is it?"

"It's in here." Grandad pointed to his head. "Let me explain. If you accept that life will deal you events that will be wonderful, plus a lot of average times and also quite a few painful moments, then you gain a better understanding and develop acceptance of life. Good times are easy to deal with. Everybody loves having fun when life feels good. The majority of time people live is what you would call every day average time. They do regular things that fall into a daily pattern and time passes by without much notice being taken. However, when things go wrong and life becomes painful, that's when people struggle, they wake up and become alert. A tyre blows out or you lose your job or someone very dear to you falls ill. These moments can be tough. It's important to stay calm."

I shook my head. "I think it would be natural to get upset."

"It is. However, it's irrational if you think things through."

"But I can't see how to accept something will break down if I didn't know it was going to happen."

"Think about motor vehicles. They break down all the time. The day you purchase a new car, you stand before it feeling proud. You tell yourself this car will give you so much joy. You can picture the trips through the countryside, picnics, and cruising with the windows down. Most times, a car will give the owner pleasure. But it is a mechanical device, and like anything built with moving parts, there's always a probability the vehicle will break down. Not only is this highly likely to happen, but when it does, it often appears to happen at the worst possible moment. The truth is most things that break down happen when you are using them and so it always looks like the worst moment because in breaking down it generally upsets the rest of your planned day. If you understand and accept in advance that these scenarios are likely to happen it shouldn't be as big a drama. Few people take on board how long their car worked with no issues or a washing machine or tyres in fact everything they purchase."

He had a point. I forced myself to calm down with long, deep breaths. "I guess what you are saying makes so much sense."

"It should do, Jack. When you learn to accept things in advance, it helps you to be more understanding. You learn more when you accept in advance that things will go wrong."

"So when you talk about acceptance, you mean to accept the paintwork on our new red tractor will get scratched no matter how hard we try to look after it."

"That's it. Accept it will get scratched. Don't encourage it, but accept that it is likely to happen."

"What else, Grandad?"

"So many things. It's about looking at the life cycle of everything. The most important acceptance is death. Mankind's greatest hang-up. Few people want to confront it, even though it's the one thing out of everything that we truly know to be certain. If we discussed death more and accepted it as our fate, I believe most people would lead better, fuller lives."

I was beginning to feel uncomfortable. Grandad's words were hitting close to home. "I understand why people don't talk about it. It's not a pleasant subject."

"That's true. But maybe that's because we've hidden from it for centuries. Other cultures deal with it better than we do."

"Well, I'm not sure I want to think about it."

"I understand. But look at what you know. Everyone will die. Most people ignore it and will never discuss it. That's why it gets messy when someone passes away. Few people discuss tidying up their affairs in advance because they don't want to face the reality."

Grandad was right. No one talked about death in our house.

"Jack, when a relative advances in years and becomes sick, the family gathers around praying. Please don't let this person die. It makes no sense. What they are really saying is don't die because we will really miss you. And that's okay, because they wouldn't be human if they didn't. They've known this person most of their life. No matter what they say or do or what they pray for, they can't stop their loved one from dying. They must die – it's part of life's cycle to be born, to live and to die. The richest men and women who've ever lived have never cheated death. Medicines and machines may prolong life, but everyone has to accept that death is always just beyond the horizon."

I stared at the ground, nudging a bit of mud with my shoe. "What does accepting death do for somebody?"

"Wouldn't it be better if the family understood death? What if they held their relative's hands, sang to them and told them how much they loved them? They could thank them for being part of their lives and share with them what they meant to each other. It would be wonderful if the person dying accepted this was their time and was ready to go without fear. Family could wish them a speedy transition to the next stage, whatever that means to the individual. That would be a better send-off."

"It sounds better. Why don't we treat it in this way?"

"Because most people fear death. They find it difficult to accept that they or someone close to them will die. They keep hoping it's not true, that it will go away. This is futile. It's like praying for Monday morning not to happen. It always will. No amount of prayer can stop death from happening. Our society through its silence has unwittingly fed its citizens the fear of death, and it's wrong because there's something very beautiful within it for us all. I don't believe there is a hell, or that anyone asks you to account for yourself. For me, it's simply a transition to a new life form."

"I still don't want to believe all my family will die," I said stubbornly.

"And so, you're avoiding the reality." Grandad put down the tool he was working with, took my shoulders in his hands and gazed into my eyes. "Understand everyone special to you will die. It could be today, or in forty years, nobody knows. Not knowing is the beauty of life. Ask yourself, what would your life be like without them? That question alone should help you understand how sad your life would be. Accept that one day they will no longer be here, but don't think it is faraway. Assume every time you meet, it will be the last time. This should help you make sure every moment spent together counts. Whatever you need to say to them, say it now. Don't have regrets after-wards. Tell them how important they are while they are full of life and alive. You just might get back from them what you mean to them."

"I guess it makes sense ... but it's still an awkward subject to bring up."

"It is, but it's your job to talk about it more and change this taboo we all live with. Life can be cruel. I've lost many friends who looked healthy but died suddenly from heart attacks or a stroke. I'm fortunate because I wear my heart on my sleeve and had already told each of them how I felt. Only that way did they know how much they meant to me."

"That's awesome, Grandad. It means you wouldn't be so sad when they died."

"Don't misunderstand me: I was still sad, but not upset because we'd left nothing unsaid. They knew my love for them."

"I guess some people want to live forever."

"I'm sure they do, but I read a story once that put me off that idea. It went like this. A man found a mysterious well hidden deep within a secret valley. On the sign above the well was a sign:

Drink from me and you shall have everlasting life

"THE MAN, excited by what he had found, wound the bucket up filled with fresh water. He filled a small cup tied to the bucket and lifted it towards his lips. A crow perched on a nearby branch coughed. 'Are you sure you want this?' it asked him. The man looked at the crow, with its broken wings, a missing eye, half a beak and misshapen legs. The man asked the crow what had happened to it. The crow replied, 'I drank from this bucket a long, long time ago, and every day since, I've prayed to die, to find my peace. But I can't. I have to endure life forever, in this broken body.' The man looked at the crow and put the ladle down."

I considered this. Who would want to live forever in an ageing body? "Are you saying that death is a good thing?"

"It is, but only after you've lived life to the fullest and given it everything you've got. After that, when your time comes, embrace it."

"I never considered living too long. It doesn't sound appealing." I grew silent for a while as I thought about it. "What else should we accept?" I asked eventually.

"Possessions, Jack. Everything you gather on your journey is only stuff. Enjoy the things you find that make you happy but accept you can damage or lose them. The worry about preserving possessions can start to control people. 'Watch the good carpet, take off your shoes, don't spill your coffee.' The carpet inherits a status of importance far above its value. Family members get reprimanded. This is what happens with possessions. They come into your house and those items termed as precious can dominate how we live around them."

"Mum's like that, Grandad. Be careful with this or that."

"I know. Too much drama over a piece of shaped metal or glass. A friend once showed me their great-grandfather's watch. They kept it in a safety-deposit box because it was precious. He told me not to touch it. How silly? To give the watch its value, he should use it. If it breaks, so be it. If it gets lost, it doesn't matter. Hidden away, no one enjoys it. Possessions should not rule you. You collect them during your journey. They are not worth losing friends or family over. You can't take them with you, so enjoy them."

"Life can seem complex at times."

"No doubt. Accept life will surprise you when you least expect it."

"Surprise me?"

"Yes. Life is routine. You go to work, come home, have dinner, then relax with family. It's a routine most people live each day."

"So where's the surprise?"

"Anything interrupting the normal routine that upsets or surprises people. You could have a fall, an illness, a pet getting injured, a storm ripping off your roof, a neighbour dropping in unannounced. These things can upset people and they find it hard to cope with the change. They need to accept unexpected things will happen to them."

"I get it, Grandad. Accepting applies to everything we know."

"It does Jack. Once you accept life will serve you both pain and pleasure, all things become easier. When it's painful, know there's a reason behind it, and an opportunity for learning. Sometimes things need to go wrong so that you try new things and improve yourself. And the same goes for pleasure. This is where it is useful to understand that nothing lasts forever. Good times never last and neither do bad times. They move between each other like a pendulum. Accept the good when you are doing well and enjoying life, but know that it won't remain this way forever – it can't. When pain returns, you will expect it and accept it for what it is."

"So you're telling me that when I accept things can and will go wrong, it will reduce the pressure when life turns painful?"

"That's it, Jack. The trick is to understand and deal with it. Have a giggle to yourself because you knew things would go wrong before they happened."

We finished by putting the new wheel on. Grandad was right: we'd lost a bit of time and it had upset me when the tyre burst, but now I looked at it from the perspective of all tyres would blow or wear down eventually, it no longer seemed like such a big drama.

"Let's head to somewhere special, Grandad," I said, keen to put this episode behind me.

"Okay, we will. But first I need to go on my own journey, somewhere I've been searching for a long time. Please don't ask me where."

It wasn't like Grandad to say something like this, so I decided to leave him be. I was in no hurry and sat back, lost in my own thoughts.

SEVENTEEN

THE ROAD TO TRUTH

I was drifting in and out of a dreamlike state, thinking how this journey would impact my life, and the insights and lessons I would take back to the real world. Grandad had been such an inspiration to me my whole life, and although I knew both he and my father had shaped me into the man I was at twenty-one, it was only then I began to understand the subtleties of how he had tried to encourage my own thinking without over-influencing me. I recalled conversations we'd had when I thought he didn't have the answers to the questions I raised, but now I realised he was encouraging me to dig deep inwards and find my own answers. He would casually question me further, probing my thought processes to see if my thinking was aligned in a positive way.

We passed a massive building lit from top to bottom and finished with a luminous green triangle on top. It reminded me of the Las Vegas casino buildings I'd seen online. Twenty minutes later, we passed the same building. Grandad was slowing to check every street name. I watched in the mirror and could hear him muttering under his breath.

"Are you lost?"

"Not at all, Jack, I'm looking for something."

"Use the highway. It will be easier."

"I can't, son, this road isn't off the highway. I've looked there before."

For the next thirty minutes, we continued going round in circles. Grandad was becoming more agitated. He strained his neck, looking up and down every side street as he muttered to himself.

"At least let me help you, Grandad."

He swung the steering wheel around again. "I'll try along here."

"You've been this way already. Give me the street name and I'll find it."

Grandad harrumphed and brought his bus to a stop.

"Let me help you," I persisted.

"I wish I could, Jack, but this one isn't for you. This is a place I've searched for my entire life but never found it."

"Where is it?"

"It's the road to truth. It's the place millions search for and yet, it evades so many."

"That's funny." I began to laugh and I couldn't stop.

"What's so funny?"

"It's been beside us all night," I said, holding my sides. "I keep seeing it through the trees."

"You must be mistaken, Jack."

"I'm not!" I wiped my eyes and pointed. "The slip road is off to the side near the central reservation."

"That's not it. I would recognise it." Grandad continued his search, turning off onto roads that led nowhere. He stopped at the side of the road, exhausted. "I can't do this any more," he said, his voice trailing off. "I'd be better off at the big round-about." He yawned and stretched before patting his brow with his handkerchief.

"Why don't you let me drive?"

Grandad frowned. "I'm not sure that's a good idea."

"You don't think I can find this elusive road to truth, do you? You said when a person needs help, others should help them take control."

"You're right, I did. Can you handle my bus, Jack?"

"Let me try. I've driven tractors before, so I reckon I can handle your bus."

"Okay, give it your best shot. We've nothing to lose."

Grandad moved to the navigator's seat, while I took over the controls of the bus. It felt like it was made for me. I altered the seat height to reach the pedals comfortably. I turned the ignition key, and the bus roared into life.

"Treat her with care and be careful of the other users on the road," Grandad advised me.

I revved the engine and tentatively drove his bus forward. "She's very smooth to handle."

After a minute or so, Grandad visibly relaxed. "Your driving's improving. It must be all my teaching." He grinned. "Take me to the road of truth, Jack."

"Let me get used to it first." I pointed the bus towards a group of trees. "The road is through there." I let go of the steering wheel, and the bus trundled forward.

There was a sharp intake of breath from Grandad. "Careful, you'll crash."

I raised my hand to silence him. "Sometimes you need to let go," I said, feeling wise beyond my years. "It must be this place that's affecting me. Trust your bus will find its way."

Grandad's bus bounced onto the verge, jostling us.

"Jack, the people on the sidewalk!"

"I see them."

Seconds before we reached the people, our bus slowed down, swinging through a gap in the hedge. We joined the widest road we'd travelled on. Lit up with brilliant white lights, it ran straight and far into the distance.

"Look, Grandad. It's so wide and with very few buses!"

Grandad smiled. "Well done, son. This is the road those other buses were searching for."

"Why can't they find it?"

"Because it's Truth Street. A place many will seek but very few will ever find."

I watched the scene unfold. The view was beautiful. The buildings were perfect. Sidewalks brimmed with flowers, public parks thronged with people laughing and playing. Leaving the bus to drive itself, I headed to the back and wiped the condensation from the window. The road was quiet. I returned to the controls.

"It's not as busy as I thought it would be," I said.

"It's not. But it will be ... one day."

"Why is it so quiet?"

"Good question. Why do people not seek the truth? Why do they live fake lives trying to convince others they are good people, while they scheme in the background? Why don't they try to live a life true to their hearts that gives you everything?"

"Everything?"

"Yes. This way is available to everybody who wants it. So many waste their lives deceiving others."

"Why, Grandad?"

"They can't face who they are, so they live in a fantasy world of dreams and deception instead of seeking their truth. It's a crime for sure for anyone given this gift of life. If they followed their hearts, they would find a far better life."

"Why did I see Truth Street and you couldn't? What does it say about us?"

"It tells me of your innocence. You've avoided corruption from others and society so far. You accept things as they are.

You're not living society's lies and whispers the way I did. You saw the road of truth because you live that way."

"So why couldn't you find it?"

"I've told you about me. How I lived and how I changed. But I still led a life that wasn't true to myself."

"Why did you come here, then?"

"I have to visit the fountain. I've a few things to lay bare."

"But which fountain, Grandad?" I pointed my arm and swung it around in a semi-circle. Hundreds of fountains lined each side of the road.

"When I see it, I will recognise it," he assured me. Similar to our tree, Jack. It will stand out."

I changed the destination board.

THE FOUNTAIN OF TRUTH

THE BUS TOOK on a life of its own and drove a few hundred yards before stopping in an unlit area next to a towering hedge.

Grandad looked at me. "Sometimes it's useful to have someone smarter than yourself on a road trip with you. I'm glad you're here. I probably would have searched for hours."

"I'll come and visit the fountain with you."

"You can't, Jack, this one is personal for me. My life's journey has led me to this moment. I think I should travel the last part alone."

Grandad stepped off the bus. Ahead was an enormous fountain, with thousands of people gathered around it. Springs spouted from statues of angels and mythical creatures, all lit in red, violet and green. The fountain was impressive in all its grandeur. Grandad tried to clear his dry throat.

"Go on, Grandad, this is your moment," I urged him.

Hesitantly, Grandad walked towards the crowds. I lost sight of him as he disappeared into the crowd. Time ticked by slowly and I grew anxious, weighing up whether to continue waiting or if I should go out and find him. I knew he's be fine and was probably chatting to others. I people watched for another half hour and got up out of my seat to find him when his face appeared at the door. He was grinning from ear to ear.

"I thought you'd changed your mind, Grandad," I said, climbing down the steps to greet him. "You took forever. I was getting worried. Was the fountain of truth everything you dreamed it would be?"

"It was Jack, and a lot more besides."

"Can you tell me what happened?"

Grandad considered this for a moment, then nodded. "I was thirsty. A little way away from the great fountain I found a small water fountain with a lion's head above it, set into a wall. I leaned over and pressed the lever. Cold water filled my mouth. It felt refreshing. I drank more and stared at the water as it circled down the drain. Then I heard a voice, coming directly from the fountain. 'At last, you've found me,' it said.

"I stepped back. 'Who are you?' I asked.

"'I am truth,' replied the fountain. 'The one you've been searching for.'

"'But you can't be. I can see the fountain over there.'

"'Ha! I placed the larger fountain there for those who need a show, the ones who need fakery in their lives. Even though they've arrived on my doorstep, they still doubt I exist. They're not true believers, nor will they ever be. I give them a fountain to satisfy their shallowness.'

"I wasn't sure about this at all. 'How would I know you are the truth?' I asked.

"'You don't, but you should recognise me. I've listened to you and we've met on a few occasions when you called.'

"I apologised and assured the voice I didn't doubt its existence. I studied the engraving on the small plaque on the fountain.

To all who search: you will find your truth in silence

"'Do you have a question for me?' said the voice.

"I thought about this, then said, 'Why couldn't I live my life true to my feelings and beliefs?'

The fountain glowed. "'Your generation didn't stand a chance. Your daily diet was guilt. Your parents didn't raise you with an open mind or help you seek the truth. They filled your head with prejudices, which they too learned from childhood. Never once did they ask you what you thought. They guided you with good intentions, but it was wrong in so many ways.'

"I nodded. 'I fought it once I had a better understanding. Although it was a bit late in my life.'

"'You did. You tried hard, but you couldn't take the final step. You didn't have enough faith in yourself. Don't feel bad. Few people arrive here unblemished. Original thinkers who spotted what was wrong carved their individual paths. Those who had differing views from their society had to live a lie to work or they would be snubbed. The important thing is you woke up. You changed your thinking and were trying to fix your position. That's why you are here: because you understood the difference. I'm here to free you from your doubt. You can finish your journey now. Take another drink from me. It will clear your mind.'

"I drank some more. The cold water rushed into my body. Energy coursed through my veins and my head cleared, giving me a true insight into right and wrong. I even washed my hands in the fountain. 'Thank you for helping me,' I said. 'Life's clearer than ever.'

"'That's all I try to give: clarity. Pass it on. Make sure your grandson learns what you failed to. Tell him to follow his heart.'"

Grandad stopped his story and our eyes met. He placed his hand over his heart and nodded to me. A moment of true understanding passed between us.

"What happened then?" I asked softly.

"I told the fountain that you were already ahead of me."

"I see," I said.

"The fountain told me it preferred no one knew its true location, so that only true seekers could find it," Grandad continued. "It instructed me to stand in front of the centrepiece fountain for a minute or two as a decoy. I moved to the large fountain, where people came and drank, some screaming and shaking. They fell back for others to catch them. I shook my head as these seekers created false, over-dramatic scenes, pretending to have found the truth. I knew this was not the truth. My eyes were clear. And then I returned to you."

I gazed through the window at the great fountain, searching for the smaller one, hidden away. "Can I go to it?"

"Not today. Leave it for when your time is right."

"Okay, I'll revisit in future years."

"Set the destination. We're moving on." Grandad tipped his hat back and wiped his brow with his handkerchief. He stood up and looked into the destination roller with all its names printed on it.

"Are there enough destinations left in there, Grandad?"

"That's the wonderful thing about life, Jack, you can keep

looking for new destinations or changing direction all the way to the end. Your choices are unlimited."

"Not really. I'm pretty stuck when it comes to choices, managing the farm and all that."

Grandad stared at me. "No, son, you are limiting yourself."

I looked at him, unsure of what he meant.

He turned the destination board and closed the hatch.

"Where did you choose, Grandad?"

"A place to help you make better choices."

I jumped off the bus and walked around to the front. Grandad was smiling down at me. My eyes searched the next destination:

FAMILY GUILT

EIGHTEEN

FAMILY GUILT

We headed off down the road. There was less traffic than earlier.

"Grandad, have you noticed the closer we get to our destination, how many more of our family and friends have appeared on your bus?"

Grandad looked up to see passengers sitting in the rows behind him. He waved to them. "I did, son. It shows how much I mean to them and how they're thinking of me."

"It's humbling to know people are thinking of you."

"Families always pull together in times like these. When they heard I was in hospital, they called each other and spread the word. Many hadn't spoken for years. My situation will bring them closer. It's time for them to remember the importance of family."

"They must think a lot of you."

"I'm sure they do, just as I do them."

I sighed. "I guess Mum will give me a lecture and a whole new set of rules when I arrive back."

Grandad laughed. "It's only natural. It's a mother's instinct to keep you safe. She thinks she knows best and probably does."

"She wants me to attend college to study agriculture. She said it will stop me from wandering off."

"Is that what you want to do?"

"I suppose. Mum and Dad are always making comments like 'When you take over the farm...'"

"Well, it's a good life, if you like being outdoors, fixing machinery and hard work. But deep down inside, is it what you really want?"

"I'm not sure. Like you, I've always wanted to travel. Being tied down is an issue for me."

"It can be difficult. Your life is never your own especially when looking after livestock and crops. You know how big a demand they are of our time."

"But if I don't become a farmer, Mum and Dad would be so upset. Our farm has passed down for generations."

Grandad nodded slowly. "Undoubtedly, they would but don't accept that just because we were all farmers you should fall in line and be one too. This type of family pressure is unfair. I've heard my own friends put pressure on their children by declaring how their siblings all managed straight As in their exams and it was imperative that they didn't let the family down, by failing or achieving lower grades. That's a terrible pressure to put on anyone. It's the same as when a family has served in the armed forces or all have been lawyers or doctors. That's families forcing their career choices onto their children. Follow your dreams and what's in your heart, not what others want. You may want to be a farmer, and that's great if you do. If you'd rather be something else, then do the thing that will make you happy. Your choice, your life and your happiness."

"I would feel so guilty saying no to taking on the family farm."

"That's the problem, Jack. Guilt is the biggest hurdle your family can put in front of you. Don't fall into the trap of giving in to it. It's so easy for parents to influence you through guilt by asking who would run the farm if you don't. They'll tell you how their land has passed down four generations and how we will lose the family name, everything built over the years will go because of you."

"Wouldn't that be true if I didn't take it on?"

"It would mean changes, but that doesn't mean other options aren't available. Your parents could sell the farm and retire to a cottage off the farm. They could bring in an outside manager or they could lease the farm to other farmers. The management of the farm need not land on your shoulders."

"I understand. But would my parents? They've mentioned it since I was a child."

"That's true, because it's what they expect from their lives. They will also throw in more guilt, for example saying your great-great-grandfather will turn in his grave. Take note, Jack, your great-great-grandfather lived more than a hundred years ago and is someone you never met. He died long before you were born, and yet his life decision to be a farmer might be used against you to influence your life's direction today. How stupid is that? If you had met him, you might not even like him. It's also worth noting that this distant relative may wish he'd never started his farm. He may have broken the tradition of his great-great-grandfather. Nobody tells you what lineage he broke when starting his farm. Maybe originally his family was a seafaring family, and he changed direction. He may have given up being at sea and wanted to work on dry land. They may all have hated him for it. But whatever he did, he did it for himself. You must do what is right for you, no matter how painful. Don't live a dead man's dream."

I was surprised when the tears flowed from me. What Grandad had revealed shocked me to my core. I had more or less resigned myself to running the farm. Now it looked like I had choices. I could discuss my future with my parents. One thing was sure: if I ever had children, I would allow them to choose the life they wanted and not be coerced into a family business.

"Thanks, Grandad, I wish Mum or Dad had raised this discussion. I accepted my fate as written as I didn't want to let any of you down."

Grandad reached forward, grabbed my collar and stared into my eyes. "You'll never let me down by choosing your own direction. Your life is yours. No one else should ever control the goals you set yourself. Remember, so many people live a life that's wrong for them. They're trapped. They have a loyalty to their family, which in a way is understandable. After all, the family has provided for them since birth. But no contract was written when you were born specifying they would only raise you and spend money on you as long as you dedicated the rest of your life to the family business. Any other business where the owners don't have children, they sell it. What's the difference?"

"I get it, Grandad. When it comes to my career, I should find my passion, the thing I enjoy most and want to do. If it's working in the family business and I want to, fine. If I don't, I should still follow my dream, while helping my family find a solution."

"You've hit the nail on the head, Jack."

I felt such a great sense of relief. "I'm glad we're on this trip together," I said, grinning at Grandad.

"I'm glad too, Jack. It will be a tough decision to make in the coming years. I'm advising you only of one thing and that is to follow your heart. Forget what we all do. Do what's right for you. If you try to please others, you will hate your life and one day you'll be sitting there asking why you sold yourself out. Never compromise with your life. Explain to them what this all means to you, and you might walk away unscathed. You can hope your parents are open-minded and accept what you want from life and support your decision. But remember, no matter how hard you try, you will rarely please others. If you can please yourself, at least one person will be happy. You are the most important person in your life, and you need to understand this and live it."

I turned his words over in my head. "Isn't it selfish if I live only to please myself?"

"Jack, the only person present in your life every minute of every day is you. If you want to call looking after your future selfish, that's up to you. One day your mum and dad will no longer be here. Why work to please them when you may live another forty years without them? If you give in to your family's demands, you will lose out on so many exciting experiences, and you won't spread your wings in the way you would choose. Never forget this conversation, Jack. You must ask yourself the crucial question."

"Is this true to me?" I said.

"Spot on. Is this true to me? If not, don't do it. Your choices must make your soul dance and your heart sing. If you don't live life to the full, you are wasting the gift of life itself."

"I'll need to give this deeper thought and step carefully. I don't want to create a family rift and be left homeless, relying on my friends."

Grandad laughed. "Don't be silly! All will be well, although keep your friends close just in case." He winked at me. "You know, that's a subject we've not really discussed properly."

"What is?"

"Friends and friendship. Let's head there."

He turned the handles once again:

FRIENDS

NINETEEN

FRIENDS

Over the next hour or so, several of Grandad's friends climbed aboard his bus. He smiled as they waved or patted him on the shoulder. He'd known many of them since he was a boy.

"I see your friends have appeared, Grandad," I said.

"I know. Friends are very important, sometimes more so than family."

"Really?"

"Of course. You don't choose your family; you are born into that circle of people. Some of our wayward cousins are a bit ... let's say 'strange'. You and I both know we wouldn't choose to spend time with them if it wasn't for family gatherings. With friends it's different. You want them to be part of your life and you want to see them to do things together."

"That's true."

"Some friends may come in and out of your life but they will always be there for you if you need them. You'll create many of your best memories with them. You'll know when you first meet if you instantly have the same desire to be together. Life is truly wonderful for those who find real friends."

"I hope I do."

"I'm sure you will. Follow your intuition, but accept in advance that sometimes you'll get it wrong. You may like someone and later find out they are dishonest. It's important you get rid of them quickly and ask them to leave."

I wondered how awkward it would be to ask someone you were friendly with not to come back again. I asked Grandad.

"It might feel awkward, but if they stay on your bus longer than they should, it only brings pain and builds more tension. Make firm decisions and ask if the friendship feels true. If it doesn't, let them go. Make a promise to yourself to drop uncomfortable things from your life. The less negativity, the less stress in your life."

"I wouldn't keep friends who disrespected others." In fact, I couldn't imagine making friends with them in the first place, but Grandad had a point: I might not know the full picture at the beginning of the friendship.

"That's good. When you find the right friends, keep them for life. Those you meet and have an instant liking to are like gold dust. No one ever has too many real friends. A select few is usually more than enough for anyone."

Grandad's words puzzled me. He had hundreds of friends. Everywhere we went, people stopped to talk to him.

"You've so many friends, Grandad. More than a few dozen, for sure."

Grandad laughed. "You've confused how many people I'm friendly with and how many people are my true friends. You can be friendly with hundreds of people, but real friends are not the people who only stop to talk to you on the street. They are not the ones who avoid you when you are down on your luck. Real friends appear when life has dealt you a terrible blow and you are sinking. They offer help in any way they can. That's what a genuine friend is. Friendly people will tell each other they heard you were in trouble, but they won't come to your door. It's an important difference."

"Some of my friends are really close, Grandad."

"That's great. Follow your dream and take good people along with you. If you travel the right road, your bus will always be full. Friends and family will be on and off your bus. Your relatives will always be with you in their own unique way. You will sense their presence. It's your job to send out good wishes and join your friends on their journey and help them achieve what they want from life. The more you give and help others, the more satisfying your life will be."

"Like giving your time to help them do a chore, like building a fence?"

"Exactly. But be aware that people will come on your bus whom you don't like. It's part of life. You can't like everyone, and everyone won't like you. That's how life is. Accept it. Make a quick decision and wave them on their way. You don't need the aggravation."

"I'll stick to nurturing the friends who'll be there for me. Sounds like they'll be the most valuable thing to help me on this journey."

"Spot on. Next destination, Jack."

"I'm not sure." I was trying to think where we had already been. Grandad was drumming his fingers on the steering wheel. I watched as he reset the destination board.

BE IN CHARGE OF YOURSELF

TWENTY

BE IN CHARGE OF YOURSELF

"Decide, Jack. Come off that roundabout."

"Hmm." I stared out into the distance. "I'm not sure whether to go where it's busy, quiet or to a place where it's a bit over the top. That's why I'm leaving it to you."

"But this is not my decision, Jack. Where do you want to go? I've made thousands of choices in my life, and now I'm running out of time, so I'd rather you choose."

I pointed towards a row of lights in the distance. "Okay, Grandad, head to where those lights are burning bright."

"Well done, a decision! That puts you in charge. It's important you understand you are where you are at every moment because of every previous decision you've taken. Each step only ever happens because of the previous one. You're here today because of decisions you made ten years ago, last year or today. Many decisions seem of little consequence, and yet they can turn a person's life around in the strangest of ways."

Not for the first time, I wondered how it was possible my Grandad could be so wise. "If I hadn't held on to your hand in hospital, none of this would have happened," I mused.

"That's true. Your decision to keep hold of my hand has

turned out to be significant. Do you think doing so is worth the value of this journey?"

"Definitely. This has been a life-changing event, and already I understand where I'm heading to, whereas before this trip I didn't really have a clue where I was going. Now I can set my destination board, point my bus in the right direction and go for it. My life seems simpler now."

"That's wonderful. Being in charge of yourself gives you an advantage. Many people can't decide for themselves or even set a direction. They bumble about between A to B and back again, never understanding C was always their target."

"I like your description."

Grandad grinned. "Thanks. Your life direction and the aspirations you dream of all stem from the mundane, everyday decisions you make. What time to get out of bed? Should you make your bed? Can you be bothered doing the menial chores? Yet many people stay in bed debating what time to get up. They don't make their bed or do the chores. Their house is a mess, and this causes confusion. The minor stuff overwhelms them, and they struggle to leave the house. If they can't deal with the small things, then they can't improve their lives by working on the bigger decisions."

"Do you really think it's as simple as that, Grandad?"

"Yes. We live in a world where many people are not in charge of themselves. It sounds silly, I know, but people will never move forward or grow if they can't make decisions."

"What if every decision a person made was wrong?"

"That could never happen. If successful people can't always make a right decision, I would assume that people with less success can't always make a wrong one. It's a game of mathematics. You may be surprised to learn that successful people will make far more wrong decisions than most of us."

"That can't be true. If it were, they would fail."

"That's the point. They do, all the time. The difference is they are in charge of themselves and weigh up the risks of each decision. They know the more decisions they make, the faster they will progress through the lessons learnt. They push forwards, always forwards. If something doesn't work for them, they learn and improve."

"How do we get more right than wrong?" I asked.

"Ah, the holy grail. Keep making more decisions and learn."

I thought about what Grandad was saying. There must be some truth in it. He was right when he said wrong decisions show you how not to do something but help you to refocus and try again in a new way. I was aware of my own decisions on the farm and how each time I got things wrong, I tried again in different ways to not look so silly or waste money. There was something true of learning from getting things wrong. As long as I understood the reasons why and could live with my failures. I was confident now the more decisions I made, the more my life would progress.

Grandad interrupted my thoughts. "It doesn't matter what you're aiming for. Your mission may be to get married, buy a house, or work at a different level of your profession. Be in charge and take decisive action. Ask a potential partner out for dinner, yes or no? Try to get promoted, yes or no? Put a deposit on a house, yes or no? Every decision is a calculated risk and yet necessary to move forward. Sometimes you'll step forwards and other times back. Both are progress. Use your intuition."

"You mean like my inner thoughts?"

"Yes, and your innermost feelings. Your first instinctive reaction to a situation. Often your body or mind reacts by telling you to be cautious or take a risk."

"You mean I should trust in myself."

"Yes, always. Don't leave it to others, you decide. Try not to be fearful of the outcome of your decisions. This will be your greatest strength. If you can accept you may not always make the correct decision, life becomes easier. Understand a wrong decision will not stop you getting to the next stage, it may just slow you down. If your boss won't promote you, this leads to another decision. Stay with your present company or move to another? If staying, ask what are your future chances of promotion. Should your employer say none, decide whether to stay or leave. If they promise to promote you within two years, decide if you want to wait that time. Every step you take leads to the next decision. That's how life works; it can't be any other way. Your entire life goes from one decision to the next and will never stop."

"I'm ready for it, Grandad. I understand how important it is that I'm in charge of myself and plan my goals. Failure worried me before, but now I know it will be another step towards progress."

"Fantastic, Jack. Always ask yourself, how does this decision feel? If it feels good, run with it."

We travelled along the well-lit street, amazed at all the lights.

"Illuminating," I quipped.

Grandad grinned. "Very witty."

"Next destination, Grandad."

"I've been thinking about that, but I'm not sure you are ready for this next place."

"With everything I've seen here I believe there is not much that can shock me. Unless we're heading to the Best Seat in the Universe?"

"No, not yet. This destination is a little more complex, kind of the opposite in many ways. I wanted to take you towards death and dying, to give you a better insight."

My stomach churned. "Aren't we tempting fate? Shouldn't we be avoiding this?"

"Perhaps." Grandad sighed. "Maybe you're right. If it frightens you, maybe you're not ready and we should head elsewhere."

"I'm not frightened for me." I paused, frowning. "Okay, let's go there."

Grandad spun the handles almost all the way to the end of the huge roller blind:

DEATH AND DYING

TWENTY-ONE

DEATH AND DYING

I stared out of the window, feeling nervous. Out of the corner of my eye, I spotted a statue. It was an angel in pure white marble. As the bus slowed, I strained to get a better view. The figure was perched on top of the gatepost of a large cemetery, carved in remarkable detail. This angel rose above a sea of hands stretching upwards to reach her.

"Grandad, look at the angel. So beautiful."

"I've seen it many times. One of my favourite statues."

"Can we take a closer look?"

"Sure."

Grandad parked his bus in the cemetery car park. We stepped off and walked around the statue, inspecting the fine carving down to the minutest detail. We moved further into the cemetery, marvelling at the range of headstones and carvings. I read the inscriptions on the gravestones. Many were for older people, but I noticed several smaller graves for babies and infants. I hadn't ever thought about children dying.

"Grandad, this gravestone is for a baby who didn't even live to the age of one."

"I know, Jack. Some things are beyond words."

"This is ... tragic." I struggled to control myself as my stomach tightened. I tried to clear my head of these thoughts.

"It is, and you won't find many things more heart-wrenching than this. Unfortunately, it's a reality many families suffer every day."

"What's sad to me is these children never got the chance to prove their worth to the world."

"They didn't, son. Not that they had to prove anything to anyone except to give and receive love. What matters is they were important to someone and spread some love. If a person lives to one hundred and doesn't love, these children will probably have achieved more."

I shivered, and wrapped my arms around my chest. "I wish we hadn't stopped now."

"Don't say that, Jack. It's important you see the uncomfortable truths in life and confront these things and understand the pain that others suffer. You can't ignore that this is the reality for many people. You have to learn to empathise with those who've lost a young one. All cemeteries cry out to me as both sad and happy places."

"Happy?" He surely couldn't mean that.

"Of course. The people buried here enriched our world in their own meaningful ways. Every single one mattered. These children may not have lived long, but they helped shape their families and make a difference."

This didn't sit comfortably with me. "Don't you think 'everyone makes a difference' is just one of those easy-to-say phrases that make people feel good about themselves?"

Grandad raised his eyebrows, deepening the lines etched on his forehead. "I wouldn't say so. If your mother had never been born, my life would have been missing the most special thing to me. All the things she taught me and the love she gave. Think about all the people she interacts with. Don't you think everyone who ever met her would be worse off is she hadn't played a part in their lives?"

"Of course. She's always had a lot of friends and she's very giving."

"Exactly. So many people have a special bond with her. If she hadn't been born, our community would have missed out on a very important person. You wouldn't have been born. Your father wouldn't be in my life either, as he only came into our family when he fell in love with your mother. Your mum has had a significant effect on our family, the community and the world. Try to understand the importance that every person born in this world means to those around them."

"I understand now you've explained it," I conceded. "I suppose you don't really see how a person fits in until you realise how life would be if they were no longer here."

We walked back to the bus. Grandad pointed back at the cemetery. "When you visit a cemetery, do so like it's a park full of beautiful flowers. These souls had the good fortune to rest together. Don't mourn or create a sad place. Don't see it as a scary or frightening place. Try to see it as something beautiful. A park, brimming with the most wonderful memories and stories from people who dared to live. Don't whisper as you walk through here. Sing out loud and be part of the cemetery celebrating life and death."

Grandad climbed behind the wheel, started the bus and we headed down the road.

"I'm still not sure about celebrating the death part, Grandad," I mumbled.

"You will. One of the most beautiful moments you can experience is when you have completed your journey. You were born onto this planet to live a fulfilled and exciting life, to help your family and others achieve their goals. By the end of your journey, if you've lived with purpose and kindness, hopefully you will have loved many people who mean so much to you and be ready to celebrate your death."

I still didn't understand. "But death is the end of everything. How can you say celebrate it?"

"When your journey is complete, it's time to go to another level. Death cleanses the world of the old, frail and sick. Life brings in our young people with fresh minds and ambition. It's the circle of life, forever evolving."

"Why do we always have to evolve?"

"Every new generation brings new ways. Better technology, greater understanding and fresh ideas. If no one ever died, the elders would maintain a world their way; they wouldn't embrace change. That's why it's healthier that the elders pass on and let the next generation bring forward their ideas. It's the perfect circle and long may it continue."

"What if the next generation's ways are no good?"

"Parents should be proud of their children for challenging the way things are and trying new things in ways they never would. They should learn from them instead of dictating to the younger generation. There will always be ways of life that are worth preserving, but fresh thinking is necessary for progress."

"I suppose. It's just that death is a scary prospect."

"That's the problem. We have taught people to fear death instead of helping them understand it. If people would accept death as a natural way of life, they would live a more fulfilled life. The assumption with most people is that death is far away, somewhere in the distant future. Death does not guarantee more time to anyone. For everyone alive, death could be an hour, a year, or a hundred years away. No one knows when their time will come. Life is here and now, not in the past or the future – now, always in this moment. It should not be something you save, or plan to live when you retire. There is no other time for life, except now. Every person should learn to live in the here and now. If people could maximise every half second to the full, then they won't have wasted what is truly the most wonderful gift."

"Aren't you scared of dying, Grandad?" The words were out of my mouth before I could stop them.

Grandad paused, then smiled at me. "No Jack, I would say apprehensive would be a better description for someone approaching death. In many ways, I think life is scarier than death. I'm at peace because I know you and your mum will be okay. I'll be sad not seeing you, but I am excited about the new journey before me. There's no point in me worrying about the next step because I can't control it. Death should be the ultimate beautiful moment, a euphoric magical climax. One to embrace, to savour, to witness and to fall into with complete trust."

I couldn't speak for a little while. "Death still scares me, Grandad," I said in a small voice.

Grandad reached over and patted my knee. "I've never feared death or dying. So many live in fear of death it ruins their lives. In a crazy sort of way, they become scared to live. They fear climbing a mountain or swimming in the ocean in case they have an accident. They become scared to live freely in case anything goes wrong. That's not living; that's tiptoeing around your life. Fear freezes you into doing nothing, and doing nothing is as good as being dead."

"I think I understand more, although it will take time for me to get my head around it and accept it."

He nodded. "Try not to fear death, Jack. Don't encourage or rush into it too soon, as that is a much bigger crime against this gift of life you have been given. Respect it. When death comes towards you, try to be alert. Witness your moment and go with it. Embrace what's in front of you for all it's worth."

"I'm not so sure, Grandad. What if I'm going to hell?"

Grandad struck the steering wheel, making me jump.

"Don't fill your head with such nonsense! Remember what I told you about man creating stories to control people?"

I nodded.

"Well, hell is one of those stories. Religious leaders spread rumours like this during times before we were as knowledgeable as we are today. If you're bad, you'll go to hell. If you're good, you'll go to heaven."

"But ... I thought that was true?"

"I don't believe so." Grandad shook his head. "It may be real to you, but my truth is different."

"So, what happens to those who're nasty if they don't go to hell?" I noticed a strange sensation, as if I were falling.

"Nothing, Jack. There's no spiritual judge keeping a scorecard of your rights and wrongs through life. Judgement comes from yourself. Your own heaven or hell is private to you. As you grow older and reflect, you'll question stupid things you've done. You may even try to block some painful memories out. If you regret how you treated people, your guilt becomes your own personal hell and it can be harsh payment for the rest of your l—"

Grandad slammed on the brakes, his bus screeching to a halt. I flew off my seat, landing beside the gearstick. I picked myself off the floor.

"What the...? Grandad, you gave me the fright of my life."

I froze. A billowing black cloud was moving towards us. It surrounded the bus.

"What the hell is this? I'm scared, Grandad."

"Don't be. It's only death."

"But why is death here? Make it leave."

"Oh no, we don't want it to go away, it has a job to do. Accept it and embrace it."

The cloud surrounded our bus, seeping in through the windows and doors. I backed myself tight into the corner of my seat. I covered my eyes and held my breath. The darkness surrounded me. Terrified, I exhaled and took a deep breath in. As I did so, I felt a strange, floating sensation. I entered a different world, one of immense beauty. Euphoria seeped into my bones. I had never felt this good before. Everywhere was bright and warm. Flowers bloomed and lush green grass felt wonderful underfoot.

The mist parted and I was startled by what I could see. My grandmother stood before me. I gazed at her, my face beaming so much my cheeks were hurting. "Grandma, you're alive!"

"I am. We're all alive, Jack. Our souls live on. We change form when we die from what we were before to what you see now. It's a beautiful transition."

"So why haven't I seen you before?"

"Well, death is a change from one state to another."

"I don't get it."

"It's like a radio station, Jack. Back home you're in the living world and the people who've passed over are on a different wavelength. You need to tune in like you've done now. Nothing is harming us; we are doing fine. Death doesn't hurt at all. It's a time to rest after many years in the living world."

"Why haven't I been able to tune in before?"

Grandma smiled. "For the same reason you haven't seen your bus. That's right, I've been listening in, following your adventures with your grandad. Learn to tune in. You may see us as spirits, while others call us ghosts and some believe in angels. I suppose it depends on how you train your mind. Anyway, this is what they call death. For me, the experience has been wonderful."

"What happens if someone dies in a terrible accident or in tragic circumstances? Surely it hurts then?"

"I don't believe so. We have ways to intervene so that death becomes painless. You should drop these thoughts and concentrate on enjoying life. Don't waste precious time on thinking about the end."

I marvelled at how beautiful she looked. "You seem to be far younger and healthier."

"I am, Jack. Unfortunately, you remember how I looked but not who I was inside. Most people never grow old inside, and you won't either, just as your Grandad is young at heart. I was always a seventeen-year-old in spirit, even when I was in my seventies. It's our bodies that wither, not our souls. Don't let those who haven't died yet put fear into you. Recall how I am now and remember how beautiful death is. Look at what you are being shown today, this insight you are being given to your life. Never worry about dying. It's a wonderful place."

"I won't, Grandma. I never knew death would be this peaceful. I blocked it from my mind. Now I know it will be okay."

"That's good, Jack. There's nothing to fear. When your grandad comes to rest, he will be in safe hands. He will be with me and his health will be in tip-top condition. So, don't mourn him. Celebrate him. You will meet him again one day."

She put her hands on my shoulders and pulled me forward and hugged me. I felt an energy radiate from her, flowing from her fingertips throughout my body. It was a strange feeling. My body began vibrating, and the sensation grew stronger until my entire body shook. The purest, brightest light filled my head, and I could see myself illuminated. I watched as the light raced through every part of my body, shooting up and down every vein to all my extremities. I believe I was being given some kind of healing. It felt amazing. I smiled at Grandma.

"You need to go back, Jack," Grandma said, cutting through my reverie. "It's not your time to be here. One day it will be and when that day comes, lie on your deathbed and welcome your last moment with all your heart."

As quickly as it had arrived, the smoke cleared from me. I

looked over and could see Grandad surrounded by the same cloud. He was sitting in his chair with his eyes closed. The biggest grin stretched across his face. I watched as the smoke disappeared from around his head. Grandad woke. He was still beaming.

"Did you see anything, Grandad?"

"Wonderful, wonderful things. Your grandma was waiting for me. She looked so good." He cleared his throat. "She is missing me. She says it won't be long now. Wasn't that just the most beautiful place and feeling? What a journey this has been."

I nodded. So many thoughts were running through my head.

"Where to next, Jack?"

Something tugged at me from the corner of my mind. "Shouldn't I be heading back to the hospital, Grandad?"

"Ah, nonsense. Let's live a little. I'm allowed my last moments of fun. A couple of extra stops won't hurt us. After that you can go back beyond the veil."

He opened the destination hatch and turned the wheel around until it stopped.

SOCIETY SQUARE

"THAT LOOKS INTERESTING, Grandad. Let's see what awaits us this time."

TWENTY-TWO

BEING PART OF SOCIETY

We arrived at a small town and Grandad drove his bus around a large square where people met and sat enjoying their evening. It was cooler than the heat of the day. Families sat on park benches while others strolled through tree-lined groves.

"Where are we, Grandad?"

"Society Square. This is where the townsfolk from the surrounding areas come to meet and discuss all kinds of topics into the early hours of the morning. This is where they keep up to date with what's happening."

"That sounds like an excellent idea."

"It's the very basis of all societies, son. These meetings have played out across every culture in the world for thousands of years since the first days when people gathered together. This is what society is. Fellow citizens agreeing to live in a way to suit the majority. But first you need to agree with the aims of the society. It has to show similar beliefs and a future path in alignment with your own."

"Why wouldn't it?"

"Well, you may not agree with what your society says or

does. If you do disagree, ask yourself if you will ever fit in. You may like most of their ideals, but perhaps in some areas you would hope to persuade them to accept new ideas. If they refuse to change, it's decision time whether to stay and fight or to move on."

"Why would our society not be agreeable to me? Also, aren't most town councils similar?"

"Jack, society at a local level won't always suit you. People move to other states or other countries where they consider the people to be more in line with their way of living."

"I wasn't aware other places could be so different."

"That's because you've never travelled. From state to state we have enormous differences. In many countries, people don't have rights like we do. In some places people can be tortured or sent to camps for speaking against their government. Would you want to live somewhere you are frightened to voice your opinion?"

"Definitely not. It's shameful some countries think it's the way to treat their own citizens."

"I honestly wish they didn't. So many countries enforce rules that are unfair or bizarre compared to our way of thinking. That's why I asked if you can fit in with your society?"

"I couldn't fit with ones like you describe."

"Me neither, son."

"I don't get this, Grandad. Why can't we all live by similar rules?"

Rules in other places may not be significantly different, but they may be enough to make you want to move. Even in small towns, local councils can vote for things you don't agree with. And when I use the word society, I mean organisations, groups or whatever you become a part of."

"Like our farmers' group?"

"Exactly. Any organisation run by a committee."

"That's just about everything. What could our town council do that we would disagree with?"

"Years ago, they wanted to build a dam and flood five or six farms. They also made plans to give people rights to walk across farmland. Changes like these would have had a direct effect on us. Demonstrations took place and before you knew it, families and neighbours either came together or resented each other. Decisions by local government can ruin communities. Thankfully, we live in a democracy where everyone gets the chance to vote and we can change things."

"Are you saying I must fit in with our society?"

"Only if it satisfies you that the people you live with have similar ideals of a fair society for all. If your town council has opposite views from you, and you disagree with most of their rules, then move on and live in a place where they show similar thinking to your own."

"I get it. I don't believe I've really taken enough of an interest in what's happening so far."

"Most people don't until one day, a decision made by a committee affects them personally. When you return to the normal world, you will see things in a different light. You may be more ambitious and ready to conquer the world and improve your community. Be aware, you can build resentment from locals who don't share your ambition and don't want change. They can prevent progress at council meetings because they fear change. Many people want things to remain as they are. When you don't align with the larger community, you can either fight for what you regard as good for the community or sometimes there's so much negativity, it's easier to move on."

"I'm realising how complex societies are."

"They are. But it is not about them, it's about you. You need to live and be where you are comfortable. If you don't agree with your town, state or country, get out. However, if you one hundred per cent truly believe in them, defend them and your lifestyle with everything you value."

We sat in the square observing the people. It was a perfect place to stop for a rest.

"You know the world is a strange place, Jack. I've never understood why people vote for a leader who wants to start wars with other countries and send their people to be killed. Why the people don't immediately oust them again and say no to war. I can't fathom this war mongering power that seems to show itself once someone is elected. Another thing to note is it is rarely the leaders or their family that go to the front line or get killed. I would make it a rule that every leader who wants to start a war has to put their own brothers, sisters and children on the front line. It would be interesting to see how those family members would quickly stop most wars from happening."

"Why would anyone want to go to war? Is it impossible for the world to live together in peace?"

"It appears that way at times. We're back to the difference of societies again. Let's move on, Jack. Set the destination board to unlearning."

I hadn't heard Grandad properly. "To where?"

"An important destination for us all."

I looked at where the board had stopped.

UNLEARNING

TWENTY-THREE

UNLEARNING

As I pondered over everything I'd seen so far, I felt I'd learned more in one day than in my entire lifetime. But now I struggled to remember how I'd got here. It was strange, a nice strange, but so different from my everyday life. I couldn't get home. I wasn't in a hurry, but it niggled at me how I would get back to the hospital. Where was the doorway? I remembered falling and flying at speed through the darkness. Was the doorway back home somewhere in the sky?

"Grandad, this experience has been a real eye opener. I'm already thinking in fresh ways for my future. But I have to tell you I don't agree with everything you've said."

"Good, I don't want you to. I want you to think for yourself, question everything and come to your own conclusions."

"But what I've learnt here and what you've told me, I feel I want to believe it."

"What I've shared with you are observations of my life and how I changed through experience. These encounters have been true to me, but may not seem right to you. That's okay. I challenged every memory and worked hard to unlearn thoughts placed in my head by others. It's taken me years to sort everything out, including many things I had accepted as truth. I'm hoping this journey will help you question everything."

"I'll try. I'm sure my family won't have told me too many untruths."

"You've hit the nail on the head, Jack. It's not lies you've been told but what others believe to be true."

"How come?"

"Let me give you an—"

"Look out!"

Grandad braked sharply. Two buses had stopped on the road. The drivers were on the street, arguing. They were circling each other as if ready to fight. We got off to see the commotion.

"Are you blind? Didn't you see me?" shouted the driver wearing a red shirt.

"Me? You drifted into my lane, almost killing me!" screamed the other.

"I signalled to change lane. It's clear I had right of way."

"You shouldn't be on the road. You're a danger to everyone."

A crowd gathered around them. Grandad walked back to his bus. He pointed to the side of his bus and smiled. "Peace and Love," he said, laughing. We climbed aboard and steered around the men who were still arguing.

"Where were we, Jack?"

"You were about to give me an example of people explaining things they believed to be fact. But it's not fact, it's a viewpoint, like those drivers. Both believe they are right. They will each tell their families their own stories."

"Spot on, Jack. And it's the same with politicians, religious people or teachers. They tell you what they believe to be true, but have they ever really questioned what they've been told, or do they just believe generation after generation? If a person has an opposing view, it's worth giving them both a fair hearing because their version will also be true. Your job is to listen to the different viewpoints and decide what feels true to you."

"What if I chose one side and later believed the other person was correct? Is it okay to change my mind?"

"If your viewpoint changes, go with it. Learn and develop with it. Understanding your viewpoint has changed is important. People who realise their thinking was wrong but don't want to admit it for fear of losing face are in the worst situation. This causes them problems. If you change, admit it. Say 'I got it wrong.' It makes for an easier road if you face your truths."

"Do I have much unlearning to do? I'm sure most things I know are true."

"That's because so far you've believed everything and had no reason to doubt anyone. No one gives you a checklist to run through all things ever told to you. Assess what you are discussing as to whether it feels true to you. I'm not saying what society has taught you so far is right or wrong, or that anyone has misled you; you are the one who will decide that. Question everything and ask if something feels true to you. When you do, it becomes enlightening. You understand your beliefs can change. This happens when you question any subject."

I said it out loud. "Does this feel true to me?"

"Yes, Jack. Intuitively, in your heart. Does it feel right to you?"

"I'll try it."

"Good. That's all one can hope for. When you ask if a view is true to you, you start a process. It will lead you to question with an open mind and raise doubts. This is normal; having doubts is a natural process. It's hard to trust your judgement, so have patience at the beginning. Unlearning and questioning everything you've ever known is difficult. It takes guts and honesty. Trying to be honest with yourself against long-held beliefs is hard. You can give yourself excuses to avoid painful answers, but you must pursue the truth no matter how hard it feels. It's a long journey and you can only move one thought at a time."

"I'm comfortable questioning everything. I look forward to discovering new viewpoints on something I once believed."

"Here's an example of something people believe but isn't true. How many times have you heard bees will sting you if you go near them?"

"Lots of people think that Grandad, but it isn't true."

"You know that, Jack, but when I was young, my mother told me many times that bees were dangerous. She wholly believed what she told me was true. She had a deep-rooted fear of bees. If a bee flew near her, she would wave her arms around and run indoors to avoid being stung. It's only natural that I developed the same fear. Whenever I saw a bee, I headed indoors. Her truth had become my truth. It was real. I hadn't been stung, and I was in my twenties, so my mother must have been right."

"But bees rarely sting people, Grandad."

He held his hand up to silence me. "I went to further education classes. One day, I was in the Garden Café having lunch. It was a trendy place with sofas. My friends and I were enjoying a coffee and some cake when I noticed hanging baskets above the tables filled with flowers. To my horror, bees were landing on the flowers. I leapt from my chair and ran indoors. Everybody stared at me. I pointed to the basket to warn them of the danger. They waved at me to come back, but I couldn't. A couple of minutes later, my friend Luke came to ask me what was wrong.

"'Can't you see the bees above your head?' I asked. He said he hadn't noticed them. I warned him he'd get stung and told him to stay with me, away from the bees. He told me not to be so silly, but eventually my friends moved indoors to appease me. One of them asked how long I had my fear of bees. 'Aren't you frightened of them?' I asked. They all shook their heads. 'But if one stung you, you'd be in agony or could die.'

"My friends looked at each other. Rhianne said a bee had stung her and it was sore, but she was okay the next day. Luke said that bees tried to avoid people rather than sting them. He explained that if a honeybee used up its sting, it would die. I was amazed.

"'Have any of your friends been stung?' asked Roan.

"'Well, nobody close to me,' I replied. 'But my mother knows people who had major problems and gone into shock.'

"'You need to talk to Mr Hotchkiss,' said Lucy. 'He's a beekeeper. His hives have thousands of bees; it's fascinating.'

"'Why would I do that?' I asked.

"'To cure your fear of bees. He's an expert and will give you factual information.'

"I left, confused. Why were they so calm with so many bees flying around them? Why did I run away? I needed answers. A week later, I passed Mr Hotchkiss's room. I knocked on his door, introduced myself and told him about my experience. He smiled.

"'Did I say something funny?' I asked.

"'Not at all. Do you mind if I ask you something?'

"'Sure.'

"'Do your parents fear bees?'

"'My mother does.'

"'I thought so. What you have is a learned behaviour not based on fact.' He explained about bees, their place on earth, how humans work and live with bees. He invited me to help him tend the hives for a few days. The thought filled me with fear and I broke out in an instant sweat. He promised I would be safe in my beekeeper outfit. Weeks later, I took his challenge. My mother tried to persuade me not to go.

"I worked with Mr Hotchkiss for two weeks. We removed the honeycomb, smoked the bees out and tidied the hives. We repainted and repositioned older hives. Mostly while using our protective suits, but a few times we worked without them. I was so used to the bees, their buzzing and landing on me I had forgotten my original fear. With every passing day, I became fascinated with how crucial a role bees played. Mr Hotchkiss told me the planet would die without bees pollinating our crops and how important it was that we supported the millions of bees by keeping them safe.

"I sat on the porch of Mr Hotchkiss's house, pleased with our work. He gave me a few jars of honey from his stockpile and explained why it was such a wonderful addition to my diet. We drank coffee and dipped our bread into a plate of honey. Bees landed on our table. He looked at me, smiling.

"'What have I done?' I asked him.

"'Oh, nothing really, except you've come a long way from the nervous student I first talked to,' he said.

"'I know. I can't believe how scared I was,' I admitted.

"'That was never your fault. No one can help it if a parent has instilled a fear in them from an early age. But you can unlearn it. It doesn't matter if it's bees, wasps, spiders or snakes. They all have their place on this planet, and it's ignorance that makes the average person misunderstand their value. If your mum had brought you here as a child, you would never have had this fear.'

"I knew without a doubt he was right. You see, Jack, that is one of society's biggest problems. People give opinions on things they don't understand. Their comments are born out of ignorance. If before you asked someone a question you asked, 'Are you qualified on this topic?' our world would be a far better place. Many things we are told come from laypeople who spout opinions without proper facts. My thoughts have always been if you want to learn about bees, ask a beekeeper. Don't listen to armchair experts; they don't understand."

I nodded. Grandad's example made good sense. "Always ask the right person, the expert in their field."

"That's it. Get rid of the nonsense placed in your head by others. What have people told you about the opposite sex, money, love, travel, business? Your quest is to dig deep and question everything for your benefit. Unlearn and relearn until it satisfies you to know you have the best answers for you. As my truth changed about bees, so did my life. I learnt that there's no shame in change. If you are not changing, you're not growing." Grandad looked out the window. "Do you get it? That was me all those years ago. How silly it all seems now."

"You've never been afraid of anything on the farm."

"I'm okay now. Years ago, I was very different until I asked the right people. Their knowledge changed everything for me."

"I'd like to learn more about something."

"What kind of thing is that?"

"I'd love to know more about hope and how it shapes us." I'd read before that hope was designed to drive us forward as people. I watched Grandad winding the handles. I was sure there must be a better way than winding back and forward – maybe a box full of letters or some kind of digital display.

"Our next stopping place, Jack."

HOPE STREET

TWENTY-FOUR

THE STREETS OF HOPE

D arkness lifted as we arrived at a new town. We approached a brightly lit street in the town centre. People dressed in the finest clothes filled the pavements. They mingled, enjoying the atmosphere of the evening. Buildings stretched high towards the sky while signs decorated the facades. Some had crosses and stars; a number had symbols I'd never seen.

"Look, Grandad, this street sign has a church cross on it. This place must be safe. What do you think?"

"I'd like to think so, Jack, but I never presume."

"The people seem friendly enough."

"I see them. I also noticed the name of the street."

"What's it called?"

Grandad pointed over to a signpost.

HOPE STREET: A PLACE FOR ALL FAITHS

"THAT'S GOOD, ISN'T IT?" I asked.

Grandad looked at me and raised his eyebrows. "I'd like to think so."

"Let's take a walk, Grandad. I've a good feeling about this place."

"Okay, let's stretch our legs. I'm getting sore on that seat. I don't recognise those temples; I'd like to have a look inside."

We travelled down the busy street. I marvelled at the buildings built on each side. Structures rising hundreds of feet towards the sky, elegantly designed and decorated. There were mosques, cathedrals and temples and other buildings that were unfamiliar. A church with a magnificent stained-glass window reflected its colours onto the faces of the passers-by. Whoever built these magnificent buildings had spared no expense in the design and materials. Exquisite marble and granite provided a framework for intricate plasterwork created by skilled craft workers. Beautiful woods carved into pillars and decorative panels that lined the walls of the corridors. Gilded statues adorned the doorways.

We visited several churches and temples. Inside people sang, some raised their hands towards the sky and the spiritual leaders at the front intoned or chanted their sermons. It felt very peaceful.

We stood at the entrance of a mosque, watching the congregation bow down towards Mecca as the imam led their prayers. In other temples members stood facing walls, others were prostrate, and in one large area thousands sat in saffron robes in total silence while monks designed pictures with coloured sands. Incense burned and I couldn't hear a sound.

After a very peaceful and reflective hour, we headed back to the bus.

"I enjoyed this stop, Grandad," I said. "It gave me a tremendous spiritual feeling visiting the various temples."

Grandad nodded. "Yes, I had the same experience. I'm glad we came here. I feel refreshed from the whole experience."

Grandad inched his bus through the bustling crowd. People paraded in the finest silk clothes, their bodies adorned with expensive jewellery. I'd never seen such wealth.

"I knew this was a good place, Grandad."

Grandad smiled. Individuals in the crowds waved at our bus and I waved back. We moved slowly as a lot of the crowd walked on the road. Some even prayed on it. It was obvious from how people dressed many faiths moved among the crowds. Nuns, priests, rabbis, Muslims, Hindus, Sikhs, Buddhists all mixed with religious scholars and seekers. They called back and forth to each other.

"It's like a carnival," I remarked.

Grandad nodded but stayed focused on the job of getting through the crowds without injuring anyone.

The street was noisy. People smiled, their hands in prayer, while others kneeled on prayer mats, bowing to their god. They prayed while a choir sang a heavenly chorus.

A man shouted, "God is great!" The people close by cheered and applauded.

Another man stood on top of a fence and shouted, "You, sir, are correct. God is great, and of course there is only one, and he is ours: The Lord God Almighty."

There were murmurings in the crowd and looks of confusion.

"No," cried a woman holding a sign, "be kind," she said "all gods are great."

"Who let a woman speak?" shouted a man. "Put her in her place! She is ignorant of these things."

A scuffle broke out in the crowd, and a man grabbed the sign, throwing it to the ground. He trampled over it.

"How dare you?" cried a holy man. "You and your family will be punished for all eternity! Your life will be worthless."

The crowd tussled, pushing against each other. A man wearing a tall hat stepped forward, raising his arms while trying to keep the peace. He addressed the crowd. "Peace brothers. Our god is the true god. But we respect your right to having a god to pray to."

A man punched the holy man. "Respect?" he yelled. "You will allow us to have our god, how gracious of you. Attack him!"

The crowd kicked and punched each other, with more joining the fight. They held innocent men and women in head-locks, arms and legs wrapped around each other as they struggled on the pavement. The peaceful street quickly resembled a war zone.

It was clearly time to leave. Grandad pushed his bus forward, but there were too many people on the road. Several tried to force their way on to our bus. Grandad pushed them off and locked the door.

The crowds used every weapon to attack the people who weren't like them. Their anger erupted and more joined the fight. A window shattered. Buddhist monks stood still while being attacked. They didn't defend themselves. A church was ablaze. Grandad revved his bus and tried to get away from the carnage. The crowds wouldn't move. An explosion rocked the street near the back of our bus.

I couldn't make sense of what was happening. "Grandad, get out of here fast!"

"I'm trying my hardest, but I can't run over them. I should have guessed something like this would happen."

"I thought this place would be peaceful, angels, heaven, God, all those sorts of things."

"That would've been nice, but I had my doubts," he said, raising his voice above the noise. "Experience has taught me religions don't accept other religions very easily. They say they love all people but can't seem to stop arguing about their different faiths. If only they could live and let live, then life would be easier for us all."

"I'm shocked, Grandad."

"I'm not. It becomes 'My god is better than yours' at playground level. Their arguments can be full of hate, the opposite of their religious teachings."

"Why can't they accept other religions exist?"

"Because if they do, they have to accept that other gods exist apart from their own. This would lead to the question of who would create these gods, therefore others must be imposters. And because religion is such an intimate journey of one's personal beliefs, followers of all faiths find it hard to reconcile and will argue and fight with their fellow human beings about whose god is the true god. Unfortunately, millions of innocents have died in the name of religion."

"That's sad, Grandad. What about love thy neighbour and turn the other cheek?"

"That's for prayer days, Jack. That's why I always say it's not God's words they are fighting over, but man's. It's impossible to fight over a total belief of love. To fight in the name of God is against everything God stands for. That's how I know it's man's words. Hundreds of years ago the religious leaders created rituals and rules to stop people questioning them."

"Which rules?"

"The people of that time were told not to question the word of God as it's written. As if because a story is 'written', it's the absolute truth. Get down, Jack!"

I ducked as an object flew towards the windscreen, and threw myself on the floor as the windscreen turned bright orange. A petrol bomb had exploded, the fire burning. Noise deafened us as people banged the sides of our bus.

"Grandad, get us out of here!"

Grandad revved the engine and pushed forward. He sped up, forcing people to jump aside. A few tried to stand firm in front of the bus, but Grandad kept his foot on the accelerator, hoping they would move aside, thankfully they did. Objects were thrown at us as we passed through. At last we broke free from the crowds and drove for ten minutes through the darkness. My heart was still pounding in my chest. We slowed at a junction and breathed a sigh of relief. There was no other traffic. Grandad found a place to park his bus and we sat for a while, composing ourselves.

It was dark. At the side of the road was a square of grass with a small white tent pitched in the middle. The grass surrounding the tent was waist high. Light shone from the opening. A feeling of calmness and peace swept over us.

We got out of the bus and walked closer. There was a sign next to the tent.

GOD

I WAS TAKEN ABACK at the sign. "Is this where God lives? Does he really exist?"

Grandad's eyes shone in the darkness. "It looks like it. The fact we talk about God means he exists, at least in our conversation. I guess it depends on what God means to you. Is he a figure who sits upon the clouds looking down on us, or like others believe, is he everywhere, surrounding us? I've heard people say he's the air we breathe, watching, guiding us and listening to our prayers."

"This could be a hoax. I'm not convinced God would live here or even if he exists."

"It's your choice, Jack. If you accept him, he exists, if you don't, he still exists because he must exist for you to reject him. The only difference is you are not a follower."

"Why isn't the angry mob back there not heading here to talk to him? He could tell them the truth and show them the way towards peace."

"That's the mystery, Jack. I suspect they fear him as he knows they live less than perfect lives. They break the rules and forget the original message of love. They completely miss what their god stood for. This is why religion is one of the strangest thing we have to deal with in life. People ignore their God because they don't want to be questioned about their own behaviour."

"Why don't the different religions follow their own teachings, Grandad?"

"Power and greed. Many of these organisations build large temples and gather hordes of money and wealth. They need not build temples to impress the ordinary man. They shouldn't collect so much money while people starve across the world. They should distribute their wealth. People from all backgrounds donate their money to help others worse off than themselves. Unfortunately so many of their donations sit in bank vaults making these institution wealthy."

"That doesn't seem right."

"It isn't. You see I believe most religions are beautiful and have something very powerful within them, a pathway for people to follow, to love, to help others and to be pure in heart. But as rules changed over the centuries from different rulers across many time periods the original heartfelt message has been lost, changed and adulterated, lost in the mire of generations of input. What started as a beautiful and pure faith in something has gone. The problem is man struggles to be content, and many among us drive agendas to control others. They say things to frighten others and twist meanings to get what they want. That's when it all falls apart."

"How can you tell its man's word and not the word of God?"

"A god of love cannot kill people or be angry. He would have a deep understanding of everything and everyone and encourage love. He wouldn't say you messed up, so I'm going to kill everyone. That's man's twisted ways."

"Is there any way we can tell what God has said?"

"No one knows for sure. However, I believe that for what any God has said you wouldn't need more than one page of text, or even a few paragraphs to communicate it. In fact, if I really think about it I'm sure he could have said everything in three simple words."

"That's not possible! How could we ever know the rules of life in just three words?"

"It's on the side of my bus, Jack. 'Peace and Love.' Tell me, what else is there to say? You can't misinterpret those words, can you? It's a guide to life for everyone."

The answer seemed so obvious as Grandad spelt it out. "Let's visit God and ask him."

"Are you sure you want to?"

"I'm curious, Grandad."

"Okay, let's see if he's home."

We waded through the waist-high grass, making a path towards the tent. The tent flap was open. We peered in. A woman sat in an armchair, knitting. She smiled.

"Visitors," she said. "How nice."

"Is this where God lives?" I asked.

"Yes, this is the house of God, young man, please enter."

"Is he in?"

The woman smiled again. "I don't know. Is he?"

I stared at Grandad, confused. "What does she mean?"

"She's saying, if you want him to be in, he is. All you have to do is believe."

"Can I see God?" I asked.

"I don't know. Can you?" The woman chuckled. "Sit down. I'll put on the kettle and get a brew going. Do you like biscuits?"

I looked to Grandad for approval and noticed a twinkle in his eye that wasn't there before. It seemed he liked the woman and her answers. I walked further into the tent. It was massive inside. It felt like I belonged.

When the tea was ready, Grandad sat on a seat beside the woman and took a sip from his cup.

She smiled at him. "You'll be visiting soon," she said. "Everything is ready." Grandad nodded as he ate a biscuit.

"I would like to meet God," I interrupted impatiently. "I have questions for him. Can you find him for me?"

"I don't think so. I think you'll need to find him yourself," said the woman. "Why don't you open the door and find out." She pointed to a large heart-shaped door behind her.

I knocked on the door and waited. Nothing happened. I knocked again. I put my ear to the door and listened before turning the door handle. No matter which way I twisted, it wouldn't budge. "This door's locked," I said.

"I don't believe so, young man. That door is always open. It doesn't even have a key. Try once more." She smiled. "You know how to unlock it."

"How? I've never visited here before."

Grandad chuckled.

"Why are you laughing, Grandad? This is not a laughing matter."

"That's because it's funny, Jack. Can't you see what our host here is saying? Open your heart. If you do, the door will move aside. Believe. Find peace and love in God."

The woman's eyes lit up. "You understand well. Many of those who pray and promise think dark thoughts; they only think of themselves. It's very sad. I see so many good people who live life spreading the word to help others. But those who fake their belief, they only lie to themselves. They put on a false show. Why?"

"That's my question," I said. "Why?"

"Because if they believed completely, they couldn't live the lives they do. They like the not so perfect path they choose. They desire to look good, so they behave in public and misbehave in private."

"Why would they do that?"

"The reasons seldom change, my dear. Greed, jealousy, hate, money and power. They say these things don't affect them, but they do. They want to live the high life and also to secure their place in heaven. But for all the things they can buy, their place in heaven is not for sale."

"So how do they get in?"

"They have to earn it. Live a better life, help others, love others. Open their hearts."

"I believe in all these things, but your door still won't open."

She nodded at me, her eyes bright. "Leave the door for now. It will open when you are ready. You've already taken the first steps by knocking on the door. Most people never get that far. Come back and try again when you're more prepared."

We thanked the woman and left.

"Peace and love," she said, waving goodbye to us.

We waved back and headed towards our bus through the long grass. I looked back. "Why is the grass so long?" I called.

"I guess not too many people make their way to my door. You think they would when my tea and biscuits are so tasty."

"I liked her," I said to Grandad once we were back aboard the bus.

"Me too," he said. "She was kind and warm, very peaceful, and it felt good to be in her presence ... didn't it?" I noticed that mischievous twinkle was still in his eye.

"Do you believe religious people will ever work together for the greater good, Grandad?"

"I would love them to, and I hope they can one day. If they could only accept that many gods and faiths exist and live and let live."

"Do other gods exist?"

"If people believe in them, they exist. It's as simple as that. They have created their god in their minds."

"Why is it hard for people to accept others are different? What does it matter if someone else believes in a different god?"

"Ah! the mystery of man. It's beyond reasonable thinking why we can't work together as a species."

"Work as a species?"

"Sure. If earth came under threat tomorrow from an asteroid or some other catastrophe, humans would bond together regardless of their beliefs to tackle their life-threatening issue. They would unite as brothers and sisters fighting to save our planet. There would be no black or white, no man or woman, no one faith against another. We would all come under the common term: humanity. My question is, why don't we act like this now and work together?"

"You need to spread your message, Grandad. It may catch on. Imagine if peace broke out."

Grandad smiled. He put his arm around my shoulder, and we walked back to his bus. "Now you are talking miracles. Maybe one day humanity will see how stupidly it has behaved."

"I hope so. Where to next?" I turned the handle on the destination board.

"You choose. Let's hope it's more peaceful than Hope Street."

"What about visiting somewhere that talks about beliefs and why we have them?"

"Intriguing, but you've just seen how beliefs affect people."

"I know, but how do you know what is true?"

"Great point. All my years working with you have not been wasted. A sensible question at last." Grandad smiled.

I grabbed him by the shoulders. "Take that back, Grandad, or you'll be leaving this bus sooner than you planned."

He burst out laughing. "That is not a threat. Okay, let's follow your nose here to find out about beliefs." He turned the handles of the destination board.

BELIEFS

TWENTY-FIVE

FALSE BELIEFS

We travelled far from Hope Street. I was quiet, pondering over my visit to the tent and what the woman had said.

"I don't get it, Grandad. I would never believe in something without questioning it."

"That's a nice sentiment, but beliefs are drip-fed into your head from a young age. It would be rare for you to recognise and question them."

"I'm sure I'd work it out. I understand how things are."

"Are you sure?"

"Yes, Grandad. I reckon I would notice if my parents had fed me ideas that weren't true."

Grandad took a blank sheet of paper from a clipboard on his dashboard. He held it in front of my face. "What colour is this paper?"

"Is this a trick question?"

"No tricks, son, serious question. What colour is this?"

"It's white, of course."

"Is it?"

"As sure as I'm sitting next to you, it's white."

"But how do you know whether your answer is true?"

"Because I know what the colour white is."

"Okay, but imagine I'd raised you on the farm and never allowed you to meet anyone else. Each day I would give you schoolwork. We would work on maths and English and art. If every day from the age of two I told you this sheet of paper was the colour black, what answer would you give me then?"

"But it's white, Grandad."

"I'm asking you a question. If for your entire life I told you this paper was black, what would your answer be?"

"I suppose my answer would be black."

"Correct. You would definitely say black. And if I let you go out into the world and meet other people who told you this paper is white, you would argue fervently to convince them it was black. Why? Because what you've been told you have no reason to doubt. It's imprinted on your mind."

I pondered this, recalling Grandad's story about his mother's bee phobia. "Where is this leading?"

"Understand that others act the same way with what they've been taught from their own family members. They are told about the family religion, who to vote for, different cultures and how their countrymen are the best. It's fundamental, like the sheet of paper. No matter how hard anyone tries to convince them away from what they understand to be true, they will argue until they are blue in the face. They know they are correct because of their long-term conditioning. They defend their position with no doubts because they believe they've been told the truth."

"But Grandad, if they are wrong, we could tell them and correct them and show them the correct answers, couldn't we?"

"We can't. How do we know what is true? What's our bias?

People must discover their own truth. They must question what they know. Their beliefs are blind faith at its best."

"What do you mean by blind faith?"

"A belief in something that can't be proven or disproven. If changing someone's beliefs were easy, life would be simpler. The people convinced this paper is black would take a lot of persuading to believe otherwise. It's part of them now. They live with other people's thoughts. It would be better if they questioned everything."

"Do you suppose it will happen?"

"Not easily. It's hard for people to question or relearn what they believe to be true. It's ingrained into their heads, so they will rarely question what they've been told. Subjects such as race, politics or the higher powers in our religious books."

"The world is so confusing, Grandad."

"It is, Jack, but it's also mysterious and wonderful." Grandad held up his sheet of paper. "What colour of paper is this?"

"I'm not sure now. You've confused me. I'm sure it's white."

"Good answer. Question everything as if it's the first time you've encountered it. Yesterday's truth may not be today's."

"Thanks, Grandad. You've given me a lot to consider."

"There are so many things to consider in life, not just our journey but the fact that every person is going through a similar process."

"Do you really think everyone has a plan?"

"No, mostly they are still waking up. They may not have a plan but they are trying to work out what life is all about. It can be difficult for them, depending on their upbringing."

"People are very different, aren't they?"

"They are. Let's make that our next destination. I always think there are four distinct types of people."

"Let's look at them, Grandad."
He spun the handle until it stopped.

FOUR KINDS OF PEOPLE

TWENTY-SIX

FOUR KINDS OF PEOPLE

The gearbox of Grandad's bus made a grinding sound as we continued our journey through unfamiliar terrain. I felt comfortable with the strange, ever-changing scenery, which differed from the fields and valleys back home. I enjoyed the new vivid landscapes changing from blue hills, orange grass and golden lakes to a myriad of other colours as we passed through.

Thousands of buses moved along the highway, a few swerving across the busy lanes and disregarding the other vehicles near them before taking the slip roads and heading off on one of the many side roads.

"It's unbelievable how many people there are. They all seem to be in a rush."

Grandad nodded. "People are always in a hurry. What you see isn't much different from back home. Very few travellers come off the highways to explore the country roads. I'm sure they get comfort from all moving together."

"Have you noticed how very few of the people here talk?" I said. "Do you think they know each other?"

"I'm sure they do. Most people focus on themselves."

I continued to watch the buses. "I wonder how many people the average person meets in their lifetime."

"That's an impossible question to answer, Jack. Thousands, probably, and those closest to my heart remained with me on my bus for the entire journey. Others I've known got on and off at various points of my life. For the rest of them, I miss a few with a heavy heart and others I'm glad to see them go."

"You can't say that."

"Why not? It's impossible to like everyone you meet."

"I'm sure that's true, Grandad, but you can't say you were glad to see them go."

"I sure can, son. I've met the most wonderful people who remain in my life today. And I've also had the misfortune to engage with others who were not as genuine as they appeared. The more time I spent with them, the more I saw the cracks in their personality; things I didn't feel comfortable with in their company."

"What things, Grandad?"

"Well, it started with minor things. They'd make unpleasant remarks, and I'd think, oh no, did they say that? As I learnt more about them, I became aware they criticised people I knew. Other things I noticed were greed and an 'out for themselves' attitude. I'm never comfortable when people focus on others in a poor light. I'd rather not be party to that discussion. I learned to distance myself from people who weren't positive, even family members who caused me pain, which was a lot harder to do. Why waste time with those who make life uncomfortable?"

"Did you tell anyone you didn't like them?"

"No. That would be rude, although I thought about it. It's wiser to take yourself out of the equation. Stop meeting the person or avoid attending the same gatherings. It's best not to encourage them or talk to them to please others. It's easier to make yourself busy and they'll eventually get the message."

"I suppose so." I paused, thinking about some of my own friendships. "It's strange, isn't it, how people come and go?"

"I think it's a natural process. My life has never been about how many people I've known. It's more about who affected me so much that I wanted them to stay in my life and who didn't, so I let them go. The quality of people you surround yourself with is so important."

"How can you tell the difference?"

"It's not that hard. Your instinct tells you. You sense that instant bond and enjoy each other's company, like I did with Bob and Joan. You learn to trust others for who they are and not whether they're popular or rich. There's no honesty in that type of friendship. It has to be heartfelt."

"Who are these important people?"

"That is the beauty of life. You never know. The world reveals a fresh adventure to us every day. It's like a theatre performance with no time for rehearsals. You must perform within your moral standards and don't do things you wouldn't be proud of. Every single person has their part to play and should do so to the best of their abilities. All these lives intertwine and act out their unique performances. With each new sunrise, it happens. People come in and out of our lives, and only the background scenery changes. It's the most wonderful adventure being part of a forever moving story. We all have days we enjoy and other days that are tough. I often think that no one promised us a life that would be easy. Each person can only be a witness to the part they play. It's their life, their gig, and they need to choose how they play."

"You make it sound like each person is in a movie."

"You've hit the nail on the head, Jack. It's similar. We each interact with people who affect our lives. Some are important and others minor. I see four distinct groups of people who affect us all, regardless of how much you interact with them. They are all part of who you are and what you become."

"Four groups? I don't understand."

"The first group is the easiest to identify, as they are your immediate family members. As soon as you are born – and if you are lucky – you are part of a family with parents, brothers, sisters and other relatives. These are family members related through blood. Everything you do from being a baby to growing old will be part of your family's story. Families share information at gatherings such as weddings and funerals, and now you and your cousins' life events are posted on social media for all the family to see. You were born into this circle and will always be a part of it. Even if you wander off, they will still talk about you. And it runs both ways. You will hear everything your family members do."

"You're right. Mum knows everything about what's going on. She gives us an update over dinner."

"All this talk builds the story of each family. This is how your community keeps up to date."

"Who else?"

"Next is the extended circle of people you get to know. These are your friends and can become the most important group to you throughout life. Friends help shape and influence you in ways your family can't. They educate you on different beliefs and new ways of living. Curiosity arises within you because of the differences between you, which shapes you far beyond what you've only known through family. Surround yourself with friends you like and can learn from."

"This feels true. My friends and I can talk about anything."

"That's good. I remember the first time I visited a friend's house. It threw me when I saw how different it was from ours. It was tidy, like a show home, whereas our farmhouse was always messy."

"It's not that much better today," I said. We both grinned. "Who else?"

"The third group of people are those you interact with. People you need to engage with. These contacts are not your friends. They have their friends and you have yours. A teacher is helpful to get you past a certain stage. A minister, scoutmaster, the person behind the counter at the store; they all played a part in your life. You might only have a minimal engagement with them, while others could be a heavy influence for several years. You talk with them; they are part of your community but are not your family or friends. They have played their part in your daily performance, no matter how brief. If you've met them, you've met them, even if it was for a fraction of a second. These encounters mean they have connected with you; they've been part of your life. They are all important – even the smallest comment, a look or a wave could influence you for several reasons."

I smiled. "You've made me think of someone I met. My lifeguard teacher trained me for two years. One week he missed our lesson and his stand-in worked with me instead. In one hour, she taught me so much about self-confidence when rescuing someone. I always hoped she would come back again, but she never did. She influenced me more than my long-term teacher."

Grandad nodded. "That's what I mean, Jack. It can be the briefest encounter but have a profound influence on you."

"So what's the last group of people?"

"The ones you may see but never communicate with. They pass you on the street, on a bus or at a football game. You watch them on TV, listen to them on the radio, drive your car on the highway next to them or people lying on a beach. They are the unknown people of your life. Strangers you never meet. Most will be fine people who lead similar lives to yours. They try to better their lives for themselves and their families. They want peace. These are strangers you never get the chance to meet, but I guarantee if you sat with most of them for a meal, you would enjoy their company."

"I understand what you mean. Sometimes I people watch on the bus if I go to the city and wonder who they are, where they are going and if any of them have amazing jobs like rocket scientists."

"I think like that too. When strangers pass you by, try giving them a smile. You can change their mood. Happiness spreads more happiness. And you can always try changing this fourth group of people into the third – those people you interact with in some way. The stranger you see at a bus stop? Try to make your encounter memorable. Talk to them and not about yourself. You know everything about yourself. It's more fun to learn about others. Ask questions. Where are they going? What are their hobbies or interests? It will make them smile and be proud they can share their story with you. And you learn a lot about them, and you learn a lot about yourself. With a five-minute talk, you can influence people, you can help them and you can give them hope or inspiration."

"Although these strangers are invisible to me, do you still think they influence me?"

"Everyone on the planet influences your life by influencing others in your life. Every interaction has a knock-on effect. Send out love and send out peace and smile to make them happy. If you want to bring the world together, spread happiness. It's contagious. When others catch it, they share it too. The more we do this, the more we help others. Maybe one day we'll all find peace."

"I'm going to watch who comes into my life."

"Only the people who help you grow. Those are the important ones."

As always, Grandad was right. "Where to next?"

He set the board once again.

EXPERT ADVICE

TWENTY-SEVEN

EXPERT ADVICE

A row of official-looking buildings loomed out of the mist in front of us. On the corner of one, a fifteen-foot-tall sign with the letter 'I' illuminated the surrounding street.

"Look, Grandad, an information kiosk. Who needs help in this place?"

"Maybe visitors like us. Although we know we are beyond the veil, we have no real clue as to where we actually are in terms of dimensions. Let's see if we can pinpoint where this existence is."

"Sounds exciting. Maybe we're on another planet."

Grandad smiled. "Don't be silly. I think we're on Earth but just on a different vibration or wavelength."

"There's only one way to find out, although I'm not sure we'll find the answer."

We pushed open a massive door and stepped inside. Stacked from floor to ceiling were books and brochures balanced higgledy-piggledy in immense columns. At the far end of the cavernous room a woman sat behind a raised desk, her head moving from side to side as she scanned the room. We walked towards her, our footsteps clicking on the marble door. She stared down towards her desk, ignoring us.

Grandad cleared his throat. "Excuse me." His voice echoed around the vast room.

The woman jumped, a startled expression on her face. She leaned so far over the high counter that I thought she would topple onto the floor. "Who are you? What do you want?"

"We're looking for information."

She eyed us up and down. "Information? There's a wealth of information in those books," she said, pointing to the columns stacked high. "History, science, places, people and a thousand other subjects. Feel free to browse and find whatever information you are looking for. It's all here."

She must have sat down then as we lost sight of her. The desk was too tall to peer over.

Grandad cleared his throat again. This time she came flying over the counter, her face level with Grandad's, making us both jump. She looked scary, her huge hair blending from grey to black with what looked like a lightning strike coming down it. Her ruby-red lipstick and thick black-rimmed glasses made her seem even more sinister.

"Sore throat?" she asked.

"No," said Grandad.

"Then why do you insist on making that strange noise?"

"I was trying to get your attention."

"Why? Can't you speak?"

Grandad looked at me and nodded towards the door.

The woman hadn't finished. "Why not try this to get my attention: 'Hello, hello, I have a question? Please can you give me the answer, oh incredible librarian of all information?'"

I stepped forward. "We're sorry. My Grandad is not used to travelling. He didn't understand your rules. Where we come from—"

The woman leapt over her desk, landing next to me. She pushed her face so close I could feel her breath on my cheeks. She prodded me with a pencil she took from behind her ear. "Explain what you mean by 'where we come from'."

"I think it's time we left." Grandad grabbed my shirt and pulled me towards the door.

"Where do you think you are going? You haven't asked your question."

"It's okay, we need to move on. Thanks for your help," I shouted.

"I've not given you any help yet. You must ask your question. That's why I am here, to answer questions. If only people knew how to ask correctly. Too many poor questions in this world. No wonder we are in the state we are."

The librarian sprinted around the room as we headed towards the door. With a hop and a skip, she leapt onto a set of tall ladders. She was singing in a high-pitched voice as she weaved between the columns of books her ladder marching from side to side like some mechanical robot. She reached the exit before us slamming the large door. She slid down the ladders, produced a key on a chain around her neck and locked us in.

"Let me be frank. Ask your question or stay here forever. Am I reaching you?" She smiled nastily.

"All we want is to know where we are," I murmured.

"Is this a trick? Where do you think you are?"

Scrambling up a ladder, she leant against a column of books. Her fingers flipped through the pages as she searched at lightning speed. Books flew over her shoulder as she worked her way down the column. Each book landed perfectly on top of each other, building a new column.

"Found it," she shouted and rushed back over beside us.

"According to my books, the answer to your question is as follows." She pointed to three words on a page.

YOU ARE HERE

"But where is here?" asked Grandad.

She pushed her nose against Grandad's. "Here is here." Her fingers tapped out each syllable on his chest. "Where else could here possibly be? Wherever you are, you are always here. Although many never remain present. They are often more there than here." She giggled.

Grandad pulled his head away from hers. "Time to go, son."

"Wait, you can't leave yet. You haven't thanked me for my incredible effort in finding your answer."

"But you didn't tell us where we are."

"I did. I told you: you are here."

"We heard you, but where is here? Which country?"

"What does it matter? People live inside their own heads. There are no countries. You can only ever be *here*." She pointed to the ground and to her head. "As long as you are here, in this moment, then you are every place you ever wanted to be."

Grandad looked tired. He was not in the mood. "We want to find the Best Seat in the Universe," he said.

"Is that the best you can do? Another trick question. Please clarify, which seat and which universe? I would say 'best' is subjective."

"I see. So how many universes are there, then?" asked Grandad.

"Once again, trying to trick me. That question doesn't have

a definitive answer. It's what I would describe as an evolving question."

"You are correct. I would like to thank you for your excellent delivery of information," said Grandad, clearly at his wits' end. "Can you please unlock the door?"

Her face contorted, and she leaned in close. "But I want you to ask me more."

"I'd love to chat, but we have to go. Thank you."

Grandad slipped the key off the woman's neck. She tried to grab the chain, but wasn't fast enough to prevent Grandad from unlocking the door. We pushed it open and stepped back onto the pavement. It felt better outside where the sun was splitting the sky.

We stared at each other. "She was over the top, Grandad," I said at last.

"She was, Jack. I think I'm getting the hang of this place. We need to find out where we are."

"I know where we are."

"Do you?"

"Yes. I thought you knew too. We are here, we are always here." I pointed to the ground and then to my head.

Grandad clapped me on the back of the head and we both laughed. "All joking aside, Jack, she raised an excellent point."

"What was that?"

"About the questions people ask. It's important people think about the knowledge they want to learn so they can ask the right questions."

"Aren't all questions good?"

"No, many of them are wasteful. You may wish to find out something important that helps you figure out your life. It could be how to start a business, or a health and fitness question, or perhaps what time of the year should you plant seeds, so you get the best crops. People need quality information, and so many experts in this world have the answers. Yet so many choose to ask their questions to random, unqualified people."

"What do you mean, random?"

"Well, people ask the wrong person for the information they need."

"Why?"

"Good question, Jack, but that's the confusion of humanity."

We sat down on a park bench, watching the strange world go by. A woman was struggling with ten dogs all wrapping themselves both ways around a tree.

Grandad started his story. "Millions of people across the world sit on park benches, in armchairs or maybe on a barstool. They sit and they wait."

"For what?"

"For someone to ask a question."

"What kind of question?"

"Any question. This is my point, Jack, it really doesn't matter what the question is. They listen and they hear someone saying the economy is in a mess. They look around, waiting for their moment. They hold back, looking calm while inside they are desperate to tell you their thoughts and dispense their free advice."

"Is there anything wrong with that?"

Grandad looked at me and shook his head. He didn't answer immediately. "I have a simple philosophy in life, Jack. I recognise people are experts in their own fields because the world needs them to solve our problems."

"Like who?"

"Well, if you have a roof that leaks, don't ask the guy down the pub, ask a roofer. If you want to know about your vehicle's engine, ask a motor mechanic."

"Ah, I see where you are coming from. Are you saying if I

want to know how a football team performed I should ask a coach and not my dad?"

"Spot on. A chef about food, a jeweller for gold or diamonds, a vet for animal health. The list goes on. What is important is that every time you ask the wrong person, you get poor answers, guesswork, information based on opinion rather than expertise. That's what the librarian was trying to tell us. She was correct. We don't know how to ask proper questions to the right people."

"Ask a farmer when to plant potatoes and how to feed them?"

"Now you are getting it. We hold back society by asking the wrong questions to the wrong people. We need to educate people. If someone wants to start a business, the best people to talk to would be businesspeople in their own specialist field. It's no good for someone who wants to open a hairdressing salon to talk to a business owner who manufactures widgets. Sure, they can give some general business advice, but even they know another salon owner knows better what will work or fail in a salon."

"What if I want to be a millionaire?"

"Ask a millionaire. No point in asking your uncle or your friend who doesn't have two dollars in his back pocket."

I nodded. "Is that why when I was in college I used a maths tutor and not my mum?"

"Correct. Your mother may know basic mathematics, but would you really trust her answers? Math teachers solve problems every day."

"I get it, Grandad."

"Follow this advice, and you will save yourself a lot of pain. Life will be far easier. Now, what's our next destination?"

I thought about this. "What would *you* like to know, Grandad?"

"I think we should look at why so many of us worry about things that rarely materialise."

"I get where you are coming from. Mum worries and stays up late if I go for a beer with the boys. No matter how many times I tell her, she sits up worrying until I get home."

"That's a mother's instinct. She's looked after you every step of the way; it's hard for her not to be protective. You should be grateful that she's concerned about you. So many don't care."

"I suppose you're right."

"Let's set the destination board." He got out of the driver's seat and wound away.

DON'T WORRY

TWENTY-EIGHT

DON'T WORRY

Grandad was smiling as he drove his bus. I wondered why he rarely seemed upset or sad.

"Don't you ever worry about things, Grandad?"

"Sure, everybody does. But I make sure my worries are worth the effort. People worry too much about things they can't control. That's when the additional stress they give themselves makes little sense."

"You mean like not getting our crops in on time."

"No, Jack. That's a process. We're in control of the fields and decide when to bring our crops in. I meant the things we can't control."

"Like what?"

"The weather, for one. As farmers we'd love to control it, but we can't, so why worry?"

"My dad's a worrier."

"He is. I've told him a thousand times not to take so many concerns upon himself. That's why I'm saying to you to have a good grasp of what you can control while driving your bus."

"I thought I was in control."

"You would like to think so. The reality is most people

aren't. If you have a sibling who wants to leave home, you have little or no control. Sure, you can try to persuade them to stay, but if they've made their minds up, then they'll leave."

"Are you saying there's little anyone can do except try to control the things they can?"

"That's it. The things that trouble you. Not the world's problems."

"I don't think I worry about the world's issues."

"We all do. Media companies push negative news towards us every day. People worry about events happening thousands of miles away. Famine, floods, hurricanes and rising temperatures. No one can control these natural events on a personal level. That's not to say collectively we can't instigate change, but worrying is futile and will only add unnecessary stress."

"Like the scorching sun today. We can't turn the temperature down; it is what it is."

"Exactly. People also worry about future events that rarely happen. What if war breaks out? What if we get flooded? What if a volcano erupts? What if, what if? What ifs are never-ending."

"What if some come true, Grandad?" I laughed as the words came out my mouth.

He shook his head. "Your concerns seem legitimate at first glance. Unusual events can affect your life, but rarely do. Ninety-nine times out of a hundred, worrying about them is causing tension for no reason."

"So, I shouldn't worry about anything."

"Exactly. Most fears develop out of ignorance. When you hear a disease is spreading worldwide, take stock. First, learn the facts about the disease. Next, trust experts from the science community and not the media. They survive by scaremongering to sell news."

"Always listen to the experts."

"That's correct. My father once told me I shouldn't worry about anything. He said, 'Arm yourself with knowledge and most scare stories will dissolve in front of you.'"

"And did you?"

"I tried, but I couldn't. I still worried about my grades, my girlfriends, my ability to work the farm – I was always nervous."

"So how did you learn to stop worrying?"

"Well, it was a strange thing. My dad kept coming back to knowledge and understanding. One day he sat me down and told me to count to ten. I thought this was strange, but I did it. He then asked if I was sure my numbers were correct. 'Of course they are,' I said. He asked me how certain I was, and I told him one hundred per cent confident. I counted them out loud in front of him. My father then asked if it was possible I'd missed a number or added in an extra one. I, of course, denied this, and counted again, a little louder.

"'You have it, son,' he said to me.

"I asked, 'What do I have? All I did was count to ten.'

"'No,' he replied. 'That's not all you did. You did far more. You were positive everything was correct. You were sure you were one hundred per cent accurate. When you know a subject inside out, that's when you have expert knowledge.'" Grandad paused.

I wasn't following this. "Let me get this straight. Your father asked you to count to ten and then told you there was nothing to worry about in your future life? That makes no sense."

"Well, sort of. What he proved to me was if your knowledge is sound, you have nothing to worry about, ever! He said if you know a subject inside out, you can be safe knowing that any actions you take based on that knowledge will deliver the correct results."

"I must be stupid. I'm still not getting this."

"When I was a young farmer, I worried about many things.

Our cattle wandering off and getting lost. Fields ploughed the wrong way and flooding our neighbour's land. Or the worst of all, not having enough food through the winter for our livestock."

"That's a lot of worries."

"It was. However, with each season I gained experience. Like counting to ten, once I gained more knowledge, I was in control. I built proper fences to keep our cattle safe. I studied the curvature of our land and ploughed our fields the correct way. I stocked extra feed and knew we could survive tough winters. My certainty came from knowledge. The more I learnt, the less I worried."

"Are you saying that knowing any subject inside out that all worries disappear?"

"Not completely, but they become far less. You won't ever be worry-free, but your knowledge removes most of the 'what if's and fills you with confidence."

"I get it. If your tractor doesn't start, you don't worry. You reach for your tools."

"Correct. Each subject is a new challenge. It's like bringing up a baby. Every new parent is fearful of this bundle of joy. As soon as it starts to cry, you try everything to get it to stop. Yet as your knowledge increases, you learn to assess things with a clearer head. The baby cries; you don't panic. You understand it wants attention. It needs to be fed or washed, or it's too hot or cold. Whatever the issue, once you apply knowledge, you can stop worrying. You learn to relax from the baby's demands. When you have a second child and it cries, the knowledge from raising the first child comes to the fore and you don't panic as much."

"But what about if the baby is ill? Wouldn't that make you worry, Grandad?"

"Of course. But you have to take a measured response

because worrying doesn't help or change your situation. A sick baby is a parent's worst nightmare and we have to recognise the limits of our knowledge. That's when it's time to visit a doctor. The doctor's job is to assess the child and take action. You will never see a doctor worry or show fear when a child is ill. They are calm and they work through a routine, ticking off the symptoms, one by one, until they deliver a diagnosis. Once a doctor has worked out the problem, they prescribe a treatment or medicine based on years of assessments. The doctor's knowledge is greater than ours. While we panic, the doctor understands the process."

"And for farmers it is the same with foul weather affecting our crops."

"Exactly. It's happened many times in my life and it will happen again."

"Did that have you worried, Grandad?"

"It did. But what could I do? When you can't control a situation, you must accept your position, that's why acceptance is important. Once crops get ruined, that's it. What does worrying achieve? Nothing. As a farmer, it's my job to plant the seeds, water, fertilise and tend to the crops as they grow. There's little any farmer can do if the weather turns against him – it's nature at its finest. When you farm, you must calculate that every eight to ten years you will have a dreadful year with no crops. If you plan in this way, you can keep a little aside each year and when the terrible year happens, and be sure it will, then your planning makes life a little easier. If you know this in advance, you can accept it, deal with it and move on. These are the challenges. Never worry about things you can't control."

"The more I learn about things, the less I will worry about them."

"Good. Knowledge takes away guesswork and uncertainty. If you understand the number seven comes after six, you know it. Having a hundred per cent positive answer would make you take the correct decision. All subjects are the same. Learn all you can."

"Thanks, Grandad. I'll not worry so much now."

"You're too young to have many worries. My dad used to say the only thing to worry about is your next heartbeat. He would then finish by saying, and if that next heartbeat doesn't happen, you have nothing to worry about, anyway."

We laughed. "Next destination, Grandad."

"A simple one this time, Jack." He set the board.

FEAR

TWENTY-NINE

OTHER PEOPLE'S FEARS

W e felt comfortable touring this strange world. It felt like home until something strange would appear before us, reminding us we were definitely in another place. We enjoyed some weird and wonderful sights of the local people gathering rainbow light in jars, conversing with trees and kids hanging precariously from kites, swirling around in the air.

We arrived at a large town and found a place to park. It was deathly quiet with no one on the streets.

I looked around and notice a window with a large yellow curtain with painted eyes peering from behind it. "Look at that, Grandad," I said, pointing. "What do you think it means?"

"I see it. It looks like someone peering from behind a curtain. Maybe the yellow is significant."

"In what way?"

"A sign of fear. People restrict how they live because of fear."

"What are they frightened of?"

"Misguided thoughts fed to them from an early age. Fear is

natural and in our makeup. It's instinctive and is a survival mechanism for every human."

"Why are there so many things to be afraid of?"

"There aren't. Few people confront actual life-threatening moments. Most unnatural fears we suffer from are from other people's heads."

"I'm not sure what you mean."

"It starts when you're young. You're told there's a ghost in the attic or the basement. Your parents tell you this little white lie to stop you exploring when they're not at home. They do so with good intentions. Dangerous chemicals, weedkillers, bleach and other things are there and not suitable for kids. They are trying to stop you from poking around where you shouldn't."

"That reminds me of my school days. We were told a ghost appeared to the last kid in the locker room."

"That's my point, Jack. It sounds innocent, but that kind of story can influence minds and create fear for years to come."

"It worked for me. I was always out the locker room first."

"But how has that affected you since? These stories bring fear, and you learn more fear through them. You build more and more because you can't see the truth. These unfounded fears seem real because of those early false stories. No one comes back to you years later to say they made it up and that there is no such thing as ghosts. You are now susceptible to being scared, which raises doubts in you when you try new things."

"Like what, Grandad?"

"Simple things like being told if you don't get the right grades you won't amount to anything."

"But that's true. Without decent grades, no one would ever hire me."

"I disagree, Jack. Grades can help, but many students who leave with little or no grades often work their way into management positions. Many business owners have never had a proper education. What they had was determination, attitude and spirit when many around them told them they would fail."

"I'm sure it would have been a lot harder for them to get started."

"Maybe, but that's just another challenge to those with ambition. If you haven't any qualifications, how can you use your abilities to beat the odds? School and exams are stepping stones, nothing more. They do not determine who you will become. Your success depends on where you point your bus. It's all in the mind."

"But surely good grades will get you a better job?"

"Perhaps. Many jobs you can't get unless you have a degree. But you can also get your grades later as an adult. School doesn't suit many kids for a variety of reasons. That's why adult education exists. If people feel the need, they can go back to night classes."

"That's what Dad did. He went to night school to study agriculture."

"That's correct. Success comes from how much determination a person has. It helps the best people stand out. I've known educated people who couldn't do a decent day's work because their attitude was wrong. I've also worked with people who've had very little education and yet they were excellent in the workplace. They were treated as stupid and told they'd never amount to much. And yet if you put them in a tractor with a field to plough, their skill level would amaze you."

"Didn't they enjoy school?"

"They couldn't. Their mindset was against them. Many kids learn by reading, writing and counting in a structured class environment. However, there are plenty of others who can't handle a formal education. They can't concentrate on instructions. They dream about painting or dancing and their teachers get angry. It's not the kid's fault; it's the way they're wired."

"You mean the way their brains work."

"Precisely. Everyone is unique. There's never been a truer saying than we are all individuals. You don't need a classroom full of students to understand that. Every parent with more than one child learned long ago how different each child is. I often wonder why the education system can't see this. Formal education treats all students the same when they aren't. Many kids can't function in a classroom and would rather learn outside where they don't feel restricted."

"But if they are not in class, the education system would become a mess."

"Why would it? The last place they want to be is in a classroom. No matter how much you tell them it's good for them, it won't help. There comes a point when they rebel and find a way that suits them. Most will do well without a degree. I've not met one person who because they didn't pass any exams in school was told 'That's it, you're no good, it's time you gave up on life now.'"

"That sound ridiculous, Grandad. But I suppose you are right, everyone, even the students who struggled while I was at school, ended up with a job."

"That's what I'm saying. Life continues with or without exam results. The world progressed before exams. People built the most beautiful temples with incredible complexities that still stand today. It was four thousand years ago the pyramids were built and not one single degree between the people who built them."

I thought about what Grandad said. I'd never thought how people had created these incredible structures without formal education. "Were you pleased when I got my grades?"

"If you want the truth, Jack, I didn't care too much. You already knew enough about the farm and how to run it. You didn't need a certificate. Your skills came from hard work and practice. I've always maintained if a person tries hard and has the right attitude, then that's all they can do. I've never bothered about the actual results as long as effort was applied."

"What if I had failed all my exams? Would that have upset you?"

"No, Jack. That's how other people react, panicking and putting more pressure on the person. I would have asked you one question: Did you try your best? If you said yes, then it's end of subject, but if you said no, I would be so disappointed. You see, the end results have never mattered to me as long as you gave it your best effort. My next question would be: What are you aiming for next? If I acted in any other way, you would lose confidence in yourself for not having the right grades and you'd feel a lesser man. You shouldn't. All it would mean is others have a certificate and you don't. Many academics have certificates, they are good at studying, remembering information and putting it back out on paper again – that's it. They may have no attitude, creativity, or practical skills to perform their job. They may even wish they were more like you. They can read and understand in theory how to do public speaking, but they may not be able to stand in front of a crowd and speak."

"What else do people fear?"

"Oh, so many things. Turn off a light and people fear the dark. They can't take the pressure of standing in a darkened room. They sweat and plead for the light to go back on. Why?"

"Fear, Grandad?"

"Yes, Jack. Built up in their heads from all the crazy talk about ghosts and sinful people. Stand back and assess what's happened. A light going out is harmless. The room you stand in hasn't changed. No one has come in. No one is hiding behind the curtains. The only change is the lightbulb is off."

"Mum gets scared when we have a power cut."

"She always has, but she shouldn't. The dark is fun. It takes time for you to adjust. Your senses become more alert. Your hearing pricks up and becomes more acute, your sense of smell more intense. Instead of understanding the darkness, people get scared. Their fears rise once again. They never learn to embrace it."

"I'm going to try standing with the lights out."

"That's good. Question everything you fear, whether it has any genuine reason to exist in your life. If you don't, you'll be in the same situation that ruined my life for several years."

"What ruined your life, Grandad? I never heard about this."

"Let me put it this way. Don't tell others your ideas and wait for their support. They will project their fears onto you."

"I'm not sure what you mean?"

"Many years ago, I planned to start a business. I wanted to open a shop selling fresh fruit and vegetables. I was excited about it. I planned it down to the minutest detail. I searched for a location and found a small shop with an open frontage. This would allow me to sell onto the street as people walked by."

"How come I've never heard this?"

"Because I try to forget about it. I made my plans and counted my savings, knowing this would be my moment. One evening, I invited all my family to my house for dinner. I was enjoying every second of my surprise that I was about to reveal. I was feeling the best I ever had. I stood up at the dinner table to make my announcement.

"'Oh no, he's getting married,' my cousin said. 'Who's the unlucky girl?'

"'Don't worry, I'm not getting married, but I have good news: I'm starting a business,' I replied. I was excited as I told them about my plans. It was my big dream, and I believed in it. I finished my story by giving them all an invitation to my store to celebrate as soon as it was open."

"It must have been an amazing moment."

"You would think so. But that evening turned in to the bleakest evening of my life. The exact opposite of what I expected."

"Why, what were you expecting?"

"I thought my family would all cheer, slap me on the back, light a cigar, wish me well and offer their help."

"Didn't they?"

"Oh, no. As I explained my plan, the room grew quieter. Their once eager faces changed. The first thing my brother said when I'd finished was I would lose all my savings. Another cousin said, 'We're not business people, we're workers. Our type are never the owners of businesses, we do what we're told.' My mother got frightened by what the others were saying and pleaded with me not to do it for the family's sake. My brother explained he knew of a man who knew everything about business. He had three fruit and veg shops, but they all failed. He said to me, 'What makes you think you can do this with no experience?'

"It was a low point, Jack. I was devastated. It was a setback I wasn't expecting. I left my dreams to one side and told my family that I wouldn't go into business if they felt so uncomfortable. They shook my hand and clapped me on the back. My mother's face shone with relief. Everyone but me enjoyed the rest of the evening. A few family members approached me and told me I had made the right decision not to go into business."

"And had you made the right decision to not go ahead with your plans, Grandad?"

"No! I made the worst decision of my life. It took me years to recover."

"But they may have been right. You might have lost your savings. Isn't that possible?"

"It is. But what are savings for, Jack? Why are they so important? You save money to do the things you want. Even if my business had failed, I would have enjoyed learning so much. It would have been fun planning my shop. Fitting it out with shelves and making my signage would have given me so much satisfaction. Seeing my name above the front door would have been a proud moment. Watching my family smile when they visited. Supplying customers and getting to know what their favourite foods are, helping them discover new types. Had I opened my business, where would my failure be? I would have learnt many lessons from my experiences."

"You would, but your family probably thought their advice was valuable."

"You're right, Jack. But the failing was mine for listening to them. I allowed other people's fears to shape my destiny. They thought money was more important than living life and gaining experience. When a good idea overwhelms you from within and feels so right, you should follow that dream. To fail doesn't matter. I would have worked out what I'd done wrong and tried again until I got the formula right."

"You may not have felt like that if you had failed."

"That's true, but it at least it would have been my failure. My family had good intentions, but they had a limited viewpoint, saying we were workers and couldn't be business owners. Anyone can become a business owner. That's what the dream is all about. Anyone can do anything when they focus their mind. I revisited my plan years later and this time I didn't let others persuade me away from what I believed in."

"You started a business?"

"I did, and it was successful. This time I told no one apart from my mother. I explained to her the business risk and told her not to worry. I opened my fruit and vegetable shop and after three months let my family into my secret, one by one. What amazed me was how proud they became. They boasted to friends and neighbours how we had a business owner in the family."

"What changed them from the previous time?"

"When I told them the first time, they were frightened even before I started. They couldn't help but make comments and recount stories of others who had failed. As a group, they convinced each other it was a terrible idea and out came their negativity. When I started the second time, I didn't tell them I was trading. When I was ready to tell them, they had no reason to be negative because the business was already doing well and making money. They got behind me and cheered me on. I sold it at a healthy profit years later."

"So you took your own route and didn't listen to other people's fears."

"That's correct. When you tell family and friends you're making a substantial change to your comfortable life, watch their fears emerge. But don't let them persuade you away from your goals. Listen to them by all means, but you make the decisions based on your feelings."

"Sounds good to me, Grandad."

"Next destination?"

"I was thinking of those who don't make it, those who struggle or falter for whatever reason. Not everyone can keep going and make life wonderful. So many just survive."

I wasn't sure where Grandad was heading with this one when I read the destination he had added to his bus.

BROKEN

THIRTY

BROKEN

"We need to push on, Jack. We've had a wonderful trip, but I need to get you to the Best Seat in the Universe as soon as possible. Try to get a few hours' sleep. It's been a strange day."

I was feeling numb and tired as we drove through the night. Grandad cranked his bus into top gear and sped along the highway. The road was far quieter than earlier, with fewer buses crowding the lanes. I couldn't stop yawning and my eyes were streaming. The warm air was making me sleepy. My head fell forward as I slipped into a dream.

I must have been sleeping for twenty minutes when Grandad pressed hard on the brakes. I jolted upright to see a bus sitting in the middle of the road with no lights on. "Look out!" I screamed, throwing my arms in front of my face.

Grandad pulled hard on his steering wheel. We swerved around the stationary vehicle, our own bus drifting out of control before Grandad managed to steer it back in his lane.

"What the hell are they doing sitting in the middle of the road?" Grandad shouted.

"It looks like they've broken down."

We parked on the grass verge, then ran back along the dark road to the vehicle, the beam from Grandad's torch waving from side to side. The driver, a woman, was slumped over the steering wheel, crying.

"Are you okay?" Grandad asked. "You gave me the fright of my life sitting in the middle of the road."

"I don't think I am. I was going somewhere, but I've forgotten where. I can't face this any more."

Grandad sat next to her. "It's okay, we all forget sometimes." He placed his arm around her shoulder and pulled her towards him. "We all live with too much pressure, my friend. Life can be tough. You can lessen the load by talking to others. It helps because you discover you are not alone."

The woman nodded. Her voice cracked as she tried to get her words out. "The longer I'm on this journey, the more exhausted I become. I never want to wake up again. My time is up."

"I understand. It's easy to feel this way, we all do at times. Life gets to us all, but your journey isn't over yet. Look at you: you've still got plenty to offer this world."

"I don't think so..."

"Of course you have. Who do you know out there who needs your help?"

Her words came out slowly each word laboured between breaths. "My grandkids I suppose ... and my local bowling club could do with my help to fix the clubhouse."

"That's a good start. So what do you need to do with the grandkids?"

"What's not to do? They need some guidance. Their mother thinks I fill their heads with nonsense. But I think they need straight-talking advice from a woman of my age. I'm stronger with them and a bit more real."

"Excellent," said Grandad. "I'm giving my grandson a few

insights to life on our journey through here. Helping him to gain a better understanding. Here he is. His name is Jack."

I hesitated, then took a step forward. "Pleased to meet you, ma'am."

The woman looked me over, then looked at Grandad. "Does he know where he's going?"

"Not completely, but he's getting there."

She lay back and closed her eyes.

"Your destination board has gone out, which would suggest you are going nowhere," Grandad said. "Let me add a place to your board and get you back on track." He turned the handles and spun the names around until it stopped.

GRANDCHILDREN

HE ALSO SET the next destination.

BOWLING CLUB

"THAT'S BETTER NOW. You have a plan again. All you have to do is follow your destination board tomorrow. Remember, the world needs people like you to help others. Let's park your bus in the lay-by and you can catch up on some sleep first."

"That would be helpful. I've been so tired in recent days."

"Haven't we all?"

Grandad helped the woman to the long row of seats at the back of her bus and covered her with a coat. He drove her bus into the lay-by and dimmed the interior lights for her. I felt proud of how he was always willing to help others, even if they appeared a bit strange. His first point was always to ask if they needed help.

"You'll be okay now," he told her. "Take your time and rest. When you wake up, follow the destinations I've set for you. You now have direction and purpose. Make the most of them."

"Thank you so much," she said. "I wish I could repay you."

"You can," said Grandad. "When you feel better, help those you mentioned."

The woman smiled. We shut her door and headed back to our bus.

"Do you think she'll be all right?" I asked.

"She'll be fine, a little tired, that's all."

"Has she broken down?"

"Yes, son. There's no shame in that. We all break down when overwhelmed. It's okay to do so. No one can remain in perfect condition all the time. At least she's talking. Problems never seem as bad if you can share them with others. It's the people who have problems and won't talk that's the bigger issue. They are the ones we all need to reach out and help."

"I'm glad she talked to you. You know how to help people."

Grandad smiled. "Okay, Jack, let's find the Best Seat in the Universe and then get you back home."

We headed off into the night, leaving the driver safely asleep in her bus. She was already in a better place.

I yawned. "I'm tired. I was just settling into my dreams when you braked."

Grandad nodded. "That's life, I'm afraid. You make a plan and it changes. You have to adapt to changing circumstances. It wasn't all about us helping the woman on the bus: it was also about her helping us, teaching us something new."

I wasn't sure what she had taught us and said so.

"Her confusion, her lack of self-worth: she was losing her focus on how important she was to those who love her. All she need was a little encouragement, someone to talk to and some rest to recharge herself. If you stay alert in all situations and look for the learning, it is always there."

"I never really saw that. I need to be more aware. All I saw was how you helped her, but I see it now."

"Let's move on. We don't have a lot of time left. We need to get you back to the hospital as soon as we can. Let's visit a few final places then send you home."

"I would love that, but I think I'll miss being here. This has been a wonderful adventure."

Grandad smiled. "It has indeed, but remember life is always about having the experience and then moving forward. The real reward is always now as you live, not later when you recall. Therefore, live this moment. When you learn to be awake, being a witness to your life every moment makes a difference." He set the board once again.

MAKING A DIFFERENCE

THIRTY-ONE

MAKING A DIFFERENCE

The sky was rainbow coloured from above the hillside to as far as the eye could see. I'd never seen anything like it. It mesmerised us.

"Don't you think it's amazing that we are just two people out of over seven billion who live on earth?" Grandad murmured.

"In what way?"

"Imagine if we had never known each other. I mean, why us? Why have we had such a special time together? Don't you wonder about things like that?"

"You're my grandad. That's why we are close and know everything about each other."

"I agree, Jack, but in a deeper, spiritual way. Why have we walked some of this path together? It makes me think you had to be in my life. How important are you and what difference have you made to this world?"

"Me? I'm not important. Compared with famous people, business people or politicians, I'm a nobody living on a farm in New England."

"Don't say that, son. Never undervalue yourself or compare

your worth against others. Just because some person achieves fame doesn't make them better than you. Why should it? For me, it's more about can you leave a lasting impression."

"Well I can't do that while I'm stuck on our farm. Who will ever know me?"

"I know you."

Grandad and I locked eyes for a long moment and I gazed at the face I'd loved all my life, noticing for the first time how his wrinkles reflected both happiness and pain.

"What do you mean, you know me?"

"Life is not about being validated by the rest of the world. It's about being recognised by one other person who you've given something of true value to. Like what you've done for me Jack. You've made an enormous difference to my life."

"I'm still not getting this, Grandad. How does knowing me make any difference?"

"Everyone makes a difference, Jack. The president, the beggar, all the people you know; they all make a difference to their community. Everyone enriches someone else's life. There's not a person born who hasn't made another person happy or smile or cry. We each impact others at certain moments in time. Fame and fortune or position in society can give some individuals greater influence en masse, however, there's nothing more powerful if you can reach out and enrich just one other person's life in this world."

"I can't see what I've done that's made a difference to anyone."

"Few people see what they bring, Jack. You have brought happiness to most people you have met. How poorer my life would be if I hadn't experienced all the things we've done together. And what have you given to your family and your friends and all the people who care for you? You've touched their lives and you can't take that back. You are forever connected to them in this whole interconnected universe. That's what making a difference means. People dream of changing the world, of becoming famous, of being remembered long after their death. But most people don't become famous. Most live quiet, unassuming lives trying to build a better life for their families. In every community exist people like you and me, the doers, the helpers, the ones who improve the living conditions for those in our own area. We fight for community centres, care for the older generations, and work hard to provide safer parks and places for children. These are the important changes ordinary everyday folks need to achieve for their hometowns. These unsung heroes shy away from the limelight, but they make a big difference."

"I never thought of it like that before."

"So same question, how important are you compared to others?"

"Not more important, maybe equal."

"That's a decent answer, Jack. Never forget it. Help others and you'll grow. A wise man once said, no one ever became poor by giving."

"Do I have to give, Grandad?"

"Always, son. Make it part of your plan and you'll receive it back many times over in happiness."

"How much do I have to give?"

"Whatever you can afford whether it's time or money. Help a friend with their shopping, run errands, fix things for neighbours. Everything you do for others may feel like small gifts to you, but they're huge to the person who receives them."

"Why would a simple chore seem like an enormous gift to anyone?"

"Because people get few offers of help. When an unselfish person gives freely with no expectations of being paid back, it can seem overwhelming that another person would take time and put effort in to help them. And remember, Jack, whatever you give out, you get back."

I thought about the broken-down woman and reflected on what Grandad had said. I'd always given my time to help my friends. I would try to do more.

"Jack, if you have nothing to give someone else, at least pass them on a smile, that too is a special gift."

I couldn't help but smile. "Where are we heading now?"

"Well ... I've been thinking a lot about how life is just perfect as it is."

"I don't know about that, Grandad. The number of things that go wrong, tractors breaking down, the bank chasing us, I wouldn't say it's perfect."

Grandad laughed. "That's exactly what I mean. Perfect."

He set the destination board.

PERFECTION

THIRTY-TWO

THE UNCARVED BLOCK

Grandad parked his bus in a lay-by overlooking a spectacular city. It differed from anything we'd seen before. Under a vast glass dome, the city sat protected from the outside world. The lights from the buildings reflected on the protective layer and lit the night sky. Streaks of lightning ran along the outside of the dome in green and purple shades. I broke the silence.

"I thought the statues in the gardens tonight were terrific."

"I agree, exquisite. Which was your favourite?"

"The one with the dragons playing."

"Yes, I liked it too. Very exciting for a wood carving. There was a lot going on."

"There was. I also liked the carving of the three horses dancing on their hind legs. I always think how incredible it is that artists can carve things out of wood and stone and make them so realistic. It would be wonderful to have these skills and produce amazing works of art."

"For sure it would. Enjoy their talents but never miss the genuine beauty that surrounds you."

"What does that mean? I'm not sure I've ever seen anything more impressive than those horses."

Grandad left the bus through the back door. He walked to the side of a garden and waited for me to join him. There, lying in the bushes, was a tangled lump of wood covered with moss. He picked it up. "Any thoughts, Jack?" He held the piece of wood in front of my face.

"It's a rotten branch." I was unimpressed.

Grandad placed his foot on a large boulder sitting at the side of the flowerbeds. "And what about this rock?"

"It's a stone, Grandad. Nothing special. Look, there are thousands scattered across the hillside."

"That's true. Notice that every one of them is different. How do these two items compare to your statues in the park?"

"Compare them to the statues? Are you serious?"

"I am."

"Well, they don't compare. They look boring. The rock isn't that exciting, and the branch is rotting away. They're not something you'd have in your house, are they?"

Grandad laughed. "I would," he said.

"You can't be serious."

"I am more serious than you'll know."

I laughed. "Stop joking with me, Grandad. Are you telling me if you could have those three horses in your living room or that rock, you would choose the rock?"

"It's not a case of one against the other. It's more a matter of you missing beauty when it stares straight at you."

I shook my head. "I don't understand. Where's the beauty?"

"The beauty is in everything around us."

"Are you sure?" I didn't see it. "That looks like a broken branch with moss on it, and the rock is grey and boring."

"You need to adjust your vision, Jack. Have you heard about the uncarved block, or wabi-sabi?"

"No, I can't say I have."

"Buddhists have a belief that everything is perfect in its present state. This rock is beautiful, perfect and natural. All its blemishes and cracks are signs of its history. In fifty years' time, it may be different, but it will always be perfect whenever it's gazed upon. In comparison, the sculpture of the horses raises opinion and division. Some say it's beautiful, others disagree. The carving would be better if only the artist had done X, Y or Z. Buddhists ask why you would carve that piece of wood in the first place, as it was beautiful in its original state. They accept it as it is."

"But you couldn't put that in your living room, could you?"

"You miss the point. I didn't say I wanted to put it in my living room, but if I did, I would love every form and feature. Look at its beauty. Take time and be part of it. Touch it. Wonder at how long it's been on this earth. It may be sixty million years old, so I'm sure over that period it has been many sizes, many shapes. Why is it in this garden? Someone must have carried it here. Why this one and not another? I wouldn't put it in my house – not because I don't like it, but because I think it should lie where nature has placed it. But if I did take it in, that would also be part of its journey. If my house falls apart in one hundred years, all my belongings will turn to dust. This rock will emerge and be part of the landscape once again. One day it will be sand lying on a beach and some kid will make a sandcastle from it, and it will change shape again."

"But what about the statues?"

"Well, they're exquisite, there's no doubt about it. These artists like to show us their skills, so enjoy them. But also you should think how beautiful the tree is before the artist carves it or makes the first cut. A branch with knots and texture and moss clinging to it. Open your eyes, Jack, and see this fantastic little world that lives in this branch."

I held the log in my hands. I'd never studied a broken piece of branch as closely as this before. I ran my fingers along the grain of the wood and wiggled them into holes where knots had fallen out. The moss and tiny mushrooms stood tall on top of the bark. It felt good and looked amazing.

"This log is wonderful, Grandad. I never noticed how beautiful it looked when you lifted it. Now it's so obvious. It has so many features I'm surprised I missed them."

"Bring it further into your being, Jack. Hold it close to you. You can sense the energy coursing through it. Try to be part of it. Touch it, smell it, taste it if you dare, stare at every part and even listen to it if you can. It has it's only life cycle to go through, and as it decays, it will change form and feed other life. The little bugs and mites who inhabit it will break it down. It will give life to many other life forms, and they will develop from it. The beauty of this branch is it will keep giving until it has transformed into something else. Everything changes from one state to the next until it eventually becomes dust. We are part of the dust of previous generations – that is why we are one with everything. Every person is perfect in their own way at every moment. They may be old and wrinkled with broken teeth and legs that don't work, or perhaps they are young and beautiful with fine features. The truth is at all stages of their lives they will be perfect. Every stage is a stage to live through and understand that perfection has to have imperfection to be perfect. All things from humans, rocks and trees are perfect at every stage of life. They don't need it confirmed by others. But they will change, they will grow and be strong and also wither and turn to dust one day as everything does. Then they will be perfect dust."

I loved what Grandad was telling me. It seemed so obvious as he told me. "Are you suggesting I shouldn't buy statues?"

Grandad laughed. "That's not what I'm saying at all. If

something catches your eye or your heart, it's okay to have it and enjoy it if that's what you want. However, try not to miss the beauty that surrounds you. Watch what nature presents to you. Embrace it, knowing it's perfect in its imperfection."

I had learnt something new that was beautiful. "Let's move on, Grandad."

"You choose, Jack, surprise me."

"Okay." I spun the handles, reading many names of the places we'd already visited. I went past one and wondered what it meant. I turned the handles the opposite way until it came back into sight again.

"What does it say?" Grandad squinted up at it.

SOLO JOURNEY

THIRTY-THREE

LIFE IS A SOLO JOURNEY

Our headlights cut through the darkness. The roads were almost silent. We were travelling through a national park, or at least that's what it looked like. I noticed Grandad's bus was swaying back and forth across the central white line.

"Why don't we stop and get something to eat, Grandad. Maybe set up a campfire. You've been driving for such a long time."

"I'm not sure we have any food, Jack."

"We have. There's a picnic basket on the luggage rack. It's filled with snacks and drinks."

Grandad slowed his bus and stopped in a forest clearing. We laid our hamper out on a blanket. Within minutes we had collected wood and had a fire blazing, pushing its orange glow up into the darkness. Grandad cradled his cup of coffee and stared at the flames. He was in storytelling mode and I didn't want to interrupt him. His eyes glazed over as he recounted stories of the scrapes he got into in his younger days. He mused over how living on a farm gave him a certain naiveness to the rest of the world. The world had been a mystery to him until

Bob and Joan had given him an insight and introduced alternative ways of thinking.

"That night I sat with Bob and Joan, they pointed out that no matter how many friends or family you have, you ultimately remain on a solo journey."

"Why a solo journey, Grandad?"

"Bob reckoned everyone had a responsibility to create their own destiny. He said that family and friends may influence you, but ultimately, you're in control of which direction to take."

"He's right, Grandad. You've always made firm decisions about what you want."

"I've tried to, but remember I told you about starting my business? My family influenced me so much I failed to take charge."

I nodded.

"Bob pointed out something I'd never noticed, even as an adult."

"What?"

"He said everything about you happens inside your head. That's where all your decision making and thoughts are. No one else knows what's going on in there and will never know no matter how much they feel they know you. This is your own private, personal space for you to work out who you are and what you want to become. He challenged me to question my inner self and understand who I am."

"In what way?"

"What did I want from life? Who could I help? But the real hardest-hitting question he asked was, if I knew I were to die in one month's time, what regrets would I have?"

I exhaled slowly. "That's a dreadful question." I didn't have the faintest idea how I'd answer it if somebody asked me.

Grandad nodded, as if he could see inside my head. "I admit it took me by surprise. But it's clever. It focused me. I said my regrets would be simple. The people I had loved but hadn't told. The projects I wish I'd finished, the friends I hadn't talked to in years. These were my regrets, and they were all important to me."

"They were good things to settle, Grandad."

"I thought so too. However, when I told Bob this, he replied, 'So why aren't you doing them now? If you miss these friends, call them. Tell people you love them now. If you have projects to do, stop wasting time and finish them.'"

"I get it. Bob's point was why are you waiting to die and have all those regrets if you can sort them out now while you're living."

"That's it, Jack. He pointed out how much time I was wasting. That's his point about life being a solo journey. These things, only you can do. And you should do them while you're alive and well, instead of waiting until it's too late."

It made sense to me. "Bob was right, Grandad. Do stuff now. Take charge of your destiny."

"Yes. Let your thoughts guide you. It's your choice to stay in this town or leave. You decide if you will marry. You choose where you work. You travel abroad or stay at home. These decisions are your path and no one else's."

I picked up a couple of logs and threw them on the blazing fire, wondering briefly if that made them less perfect or more so as they reduced to ash. I thought about what Grandad was saying.

"Jack, it's your life. Your individual road. We've already discussed how you shouldn't live your life to other people's rules. Listen to their input, but separate their aspirations and fears from yours. Stay true to yourself."

"I understand." Something was troubling me. "But Grandad, what about if you're married or have a partner?"

"Of course, you must consider them. Hopefully, before you

made that commitment you told them honestly what you are aiming for in your life so they can give you space just as you should them. Even if you're married, it's still your solo journey, Jack. Many people live with a partner and yet inside their heads they live themselves in their own personal world. Climb into that seat and own it. Use your gift of life. Control your destiny and drive forward as hard as you can. Whatever you do, don't set any limitations for your achievements, and let nothing hold you back, especially yourself."

"You've got me excited, Grandad. I'm ready to take charge and prove what I can do."

"That's good. Everyone has the chance to prove themselves. It's not equal by any means. Some have a tougher start each day for sure. But they can still try."

"Doesn't everyone want a better life?"

"No. Some are happy with what they have. Not everyone wants to climb a mountain or be an astronaut. Many want to walk a simple path. Others are lazy and waste time dreaming instead of doing. When I tell you not to let others influence your journey, the same applies to you. Don't persuade others to do things your way. They must do things for themselves. I'm pointing out the differences, as it's not for me to tell you what to do."

"What if someone asks me for my advice?"

"That's different. If someone asks for help, and you have enough expertise to do so, then that's fine, but don't tell them how to live. Your way is not their way. Advise them to aim for the best life possible with everything they've got. Tell them to believe in themselves and go for it."

Our fire had burnt out. We watched a steady stream of stars shoot across the night sky, then carried our empty hamper back to our bus.

"Let's move on, Jack."

"Where to next?"

"I was thinking we won't set a destination for once and see what happens. Let's be a bit more adventurous. Sometimes it's good to go off grid without a plan and see where you land."

And we did.

THIRTY-FOUR

LIVE STREET

W hile I was happy to see what else was here in this world of the afterlife, I was beginning to feel tired. Privately, I wondered if we'd ever find the Best Seat in the Universe. Up ahead, an enormous illuminated star floated in the sky.

"Head towards that star, Grandad."

"I thought we were going for a wander?"

"We are. This is somewhere we hadn't planned."

"Okay. The sign says Live Street. Let's hope it's not too lively, as I'm getting too old for this."

We laughed.

Grandad drove towards the floating star. He squinted because of the thousands of lightbulbs that lit up the street, making the area even brighter. Each building had strings of fairy lights and coloured ribbons decorated across their facades. The atmosphere was electric. The buildings looked like iced fancy cakes.

"This place looks fantastic, Grandad. One of our better choices."

"It is, isn't it? Look how everyone is enjoying themselves."

I raised my hand and people waved back. They were happy. But as we drew closer I noticed that children were being jostled as the crowds squeezed in. Something didn't feel right. I realised the people's faces were false. Fake smiles painted on masks. I tried to get a closer look. As I gazed around, I could see all the houses were changing colour.

"Grandad, are my eyes are seeing strange things? It looks like the houses are melting!"

Grandad nodded. The houses were indeed melting. The beautiful pastel colours of lemon and pink with white icing were now forming into streaks of red and black. The sky darkened moments before the sun disappeared behind ominous rolling clouds. I was scared.

"Not again. Let's get out of here."

Grandad struggled to see through the windscreen due to sudden condensation. Water dribbled its way down the walls, pooling on the floor. The internal bus lights flickered on and off. I tried to control my breathing. The light was too dim, blending Grandad into the shadows. I caught his reflection in the rear-view mirror and saw fear in his eyes.

"Grandad, what's wrong?" I shouted.

He didn't answer. I made my way to the front of his bus. Outside, the crowds resembled a sea of black with hoods pulled high over their heads. Many carried weapons. One figure swung a noose while another set a wooden cross ablaze. A man marched with a deliberately slow pace in front of our bus.

"What's going on? Who are they?"

"Keep back from the windows, Jack. Don't let them see you."

In the middle of the road, a fire raged, blocking our way. Grandad stopped his bus. There was no way to go around the blockade. The crowd surrounded us.

"Grandad, I'm scared."

"Me too. I think it would be true to say we've visited better places."

"What do they want?"

"These look like wicked people. Individuals who wish to make good people's lives a misery. They do all they can to frighten others, and the more they upset people, the happier they feel."

The crowd surged towards our bus. They banged on the walls and windows, and tried to force open the door. The noise was deafening. The passengers travelling with us faded back and forth. A man pounded on our door with an iron bar, making a hole through the panel. The door held firm. A loud crack came from the back of the bus. The rear window shattered, and pieces of glass scattered down the aisle. A man holding a skull on a stave climbed through the broken window.

I was startled and screamed.

"It's okay," cried Grandad over the din. "Protect yourself from evil with love. They can't touch us if we fill our heads with love."

We both thought hard about wonderful, loving moments and reminded each other about joyful times but the man still came towards us. Grandad stepped before him staring into the darkened hood. He reached out and pointed at me.

"My friend here is from beyond the veil where it is filled with light and love. Look into his eyes."

I stared at the hooded figure and saw his expression change. He wasn't quite sure what I was and backed away from me slowly. I kept pace with him pushing him backwards. He leapt out the back window and pulled others away from us.

Our bus glowed from the power of our purer thoughts, illuminating the entire street. The shadows backed off towards the side streets and alleyways, and the road cleared. Grandad navigated his bus off the street.

"What happened?" I asked. "They were nasty."

"I believe that was a manifestation of evil."

"Why would they be evil?"

"That's how some people are, they are unhappy within themselves. They spread violence, hatred and delight in cheating people. They live disconnected from what's good and never feel guilty like we would. We would be remorseful if we hurt someone – they never are."

"I don't understand how anyone could live such a life."

"You don't have to, but it's important you know they exist. Luckily, most people are well behaved. It's a small percentage who act like this."

"Why don't we lock them up?"

"You can't jail everyone. To deal with evil, stand firm and be strong. The more a community sticks together, the sooner nasty people leave. Once they can't frighten respectable people, they are powerless. The more people stand against this evil together, the fewer of these criminals will prosper."

"Do you think that's possible, Grandad?"

"It's possible. When a community gets overrun with crime, there comes a breaking point. At some point they declare enough is enough and take action, flushing out and exposing the criminals until they move on."

"I can't believe this street transformed as much as it did." I was still recovering from the shock.

"There's so much falseness, Jack. So many people wear fake smiles, a mask that's hard to see past. You believe they are genuine, but they're waiting to trick you. Business organisations and people you feel you know can put on a front. Like the name of this street: Live Street. I thought it meant being alive, enjoying life. But when the crowd surrounded us, I saw the reflection in my rear-view mirror. Live was Evil backwards. These people always twist things to deceive."

"They must feel some remorse."

"No, son. They don't care like you or I would. They have no moral conscience."

"How can they live with themselves?"

"Good people struggle if they have unintentionally done harm to others. Their conscience tells them it was wrong. Deceptive people steal and justify their actions by saying the victim had too many possessions. Although they've hurt you, they forget what they've done and move on to their next victim."

"That's not good."

"I know, but it's true. That's the world where we live. Statistically, you will be a victim at some point. Someone will target you. They will trick you, or steal something important, an item you've worked hard for. It hurts when it happens, but don't let this play an important part of your life. Get over it quickly and be more careful. Accept you were a statistic and move on. Possessions are replaceable."

"I hope if something happens, I can live with it."

"You have no alternative. People get upset about things that happened five or ten years ago. They still feel robbed or cheated. Why are they still angry about this? It's over. They need to move on."

"But they feel cheated."

"I understand. But now they are cheating themselves from enjoying their current life. They can't keep looking back. Keeping that memory alive is a bigger waste of time."

"Maybe they want someone to fix it?"

"Probably, but sometimes there's little anyone can do. You drop a glass of milk and it smashes on the floor. There's no fixing it so you have to let it go. The milk gets spoiled and the glass shatters through the milk. There's no way to salvage it. Accept it is spoilt and move on."

I nodded, glad that the manifested crowds were now behind us.

"See your life in the same way. Some unfortunate events are irreparable, like the milk. If it's a crime, report it to the police and move on. There's no point wasting any more of your present time. The sooner you accept the situation, the quicker you get on with life." He glanced in his rear-view mirror and cleared his throat. "Next destination, Jack – or should I pick this one?"

"I think you should, Grandad. My choices so far have been pretty dismal. As you said earlier, what happened to the warm light and singing angels?"

We both laughed.

Grandad set a new destination.

THE IMPORTANCE OF TIME

THIRTY-FIVE

WASTED TIME

A flickering light caught our attention off to the side in a field. Rows of buses sat side by side all pointing towards the biggest cinema screen I'd seen. Grandad indicated and swung down the exit ramp off the main carriageway.

"Looks like a drive-in movie," he said. "Let's recharge our batteries and get some rest. I wonder what's playing? Hopefully it's a classic movie night."

We picked a spot and pulled up next to a microphone. A woman came towards us, but when she saw us, she turned and made off.

"I'm not sure I've seen this film," I said. "Maybe it's a new release or something from those subscription services."

We watched as the screen changed from one film to another. Two minutes of a romance, then cartoons and then a sci-fi movie. There was no logic to it. I noticed several drivers had TV controllers. They switched programmes continually. Some slept and others rarely looked at the screen.

"This is weird, Grandad."

"I agree, let's go. I hate people wasting time like this. Live life to the full is my motto. As you get older and more settled, it's easy to get lazy. The number of people like those here who waste their lives watching television or surfing endlessly online is inexcusable."

"Television's okay, but only now and then. Some of my friends sit glued to it every night."

Grandad nodded. "A lot of my friends are the same. It's our lifestyle working all hours on the farm that's probably never got us hooked. We've never had that much time to waste while tending to our livestock. I like a bit of TV myself but I've never understood how people can waste five or six hours in one evening. As they prepare for bed, they say the programmes tonight were terrible. A whole evening wasted, for what? Doesn't that seem a crime?"

"It does, but some people have nothing else in their lives."

"I get it, but every night? They also train their kids to do the same."

"Are you trying to be like Mum, Grandad? Is this your subtle way of telling me wasting time in front of a TV or tablet is not good for me?"

"Not at all. As tools, television and the internet are valuable. They can be educational and pleasurable. But it's like an addiction where people can't do without them to the point they let them control them and miss out on real life."

"You're right. Sometimes I chill with a beer for an evening and then I get mad for wasting my time."

"Hey, there's nothing wrong with having a night off. If you want to watch a programme, do it. But try to turn it off straight after it has finished. Don't get sucked into watching one show after another, wasting time on things you hadn't planned. Do something better with your time. Play a musical instrument, learn to paint or make candles. Anything but waste time."

"Is that why you made candles, Grandad?"

"Yes. I also sew while most men can't. I can weave and knit, and I can draw and paint and make lamps from turning wood. All these skills I wasn't taught at school or by my parents. I made a promise to myself to learn one new skill each year. And each fresh experience helps me understand more. I meet people with similar interests, and we have fun and meaningful discussions. There are very few discussions in front of a television."

"That's impressive to learn so many skills. They must seem natural to you."

"Not at all. I worked hard at learning each new hobby. Each New Year I looked at all the classes and decided what I wanted to spend time learning – painting, dancing, woodwork, welding, whatever took my interest. I made a promise by the end of each year that I'd be more accomplished than I was at the beginning. It's as simple as that."

"That's such a good plan. I think I'll follow in your footsteps."

"Good for you. You'll gain far more from learning new skills than you ever will wasting time. The best part for me was the mix of skilled interesting people I met, and their teachings were immeasurable."

"I get it, Grandad, but I still like to watch TV."

He chuckled. "That's okay, everyone should make time for entertainment. We need to wind down. But time planned for relaxation differs from wasting time and feeling worthless afterwards. If people disciplined themselves a little more with their free time, they would feel more fulfilled. Anyway, on that note, let's not waste any more time here. Let's move on and see how we can make a difference in this world." Grandad set the board and smiled.

I glanced up at it, wondering where we were going now.

CHANGE THE WORLD

THIRTY-SIX

YOU CAN CHANGE THE WORLD

The road opened wide before us into a long tree-lined mall. It looked like a place where parades or massive celebrations would happen. I could visualise crowds lining the streets, watching decorated vehicles pass by. I could almost hear the marching bands and see the crowds cheering and waving flags. Indeed, we could see what looked like thousands of people gathered up ahead.

Grandad spotted the coach park and swung in beside them. "We'll travel by foot for the last part of this journey," he said.

It was a beautiful setting, and we ambled towards the far end of the mall. Ahead we saw a vivid blue light glowing from behind the tree line. A steady stream of people made their way towards it like some kind of Mecca. Crowds on the pavements cheered on the visitors. Ticker tape and confetti fell from the sky, swirling in the wind. Thousands of balloons floated above our heads with kids running to catch hold of the trailing strings. As we stepped closer to the blue glow, its brilliance enthralled us. People stopped in their tracks, mouths open, gaping at the scene in front of us.

We'd arrived at an enormous public square where you'd

expect to see statues of world heroes or fountains with synchro-nised water dancing to lights and music. Before us, the source of the mysterious blue light was revealed. When I realised what we were looking at, I fell to my knees. I reached over and took Grandad's hand.

Suspended twenty feet above the ground hovered our beauti-ful planet, earth. It must have been three hundred foot high. I watched as it turned slowly, the atmosphere shimmering around it like a halo. It was breathtaking. As I tried to accept the reality of what I was seeing, the moon appeared in dazzling yellow, orbiting our planet.

Cloud formations passed over continents and oceans. A storm raged over the Philippines while lightning streaked along the top of the clouds above North America. We stared in disbelief.

"How is this possible, Grandad? It looks like earth as seen from space."

"I think you'll find that's exactly what it is, Jack," Grandad replied quietly, his eyes not leaving the spectacle before him. "Maybe it's the creator's view."

"I can't believe we are seeing this. Are we really the care-takers of this beauty?"

Around us, the crowd drew closer to the light. Some carried placards: *Change the World*, *Feed the Children*, *Save Our Planet*, *End Poverty*, *Fight Malaria*.

Grandad left my side and walked underneath our beautiful revolving world. I followed. Every angle, every view was intoxi-cating as earth spun a few feet above our heads. As we walked around, we spotted an enormous staircase leading to a platform. It raised up and down and people queued to climb it. The plat-form manoeuvred closer to the clouds and people reached out, their hands dragging wisps of cloud behind them. While some touched the clouds, others pushed their faces into the atmosphere. I watched as people carried violet-coloured bubbles in their hands, then let them go into the atmosphere. The bubbles scattered, some separating into groups of smaller bubbles before floating down towards land. Some fell into the ocean.

"What do you think they are doing with those bubbles, Grandad?"

"Your guess is as good as mine. Let's ask the man giving them out."

We stood in line, moving slowly towards the man. He was very large and his black woollen coat made him look like a bear. He was smiling as he gave everyone a bubble. I could hear him telling them not to waste it. Above his stall, the sign read

How can YOU change the world?

ANOTHER TWENTY MINUTES PASSED, then finally it was our turn.

The man smiled at us. "Welcome, friends. Are you ready to change the world?"

"I'm not sure how this works, sir. How can someone like me change the world?" asked Grandad.

"Anyone can. Make a decision and do it."

"In what way?"

"Let me guide you. You have three choices. You can change in a way that improves yourself. You can help others to change their ways by helping them. Or, if you really want to make your mark, you can do something so fantastic that it changes the world for the benefit of humanity."

"Is it really possible for an ordinary person to change the world to benefit humanity?" I asked.

"Of course. Every change so far has only ever been made by ordinary people. There's nothing magical about it – you only need to leave yourself open to new ideas. The trick is not to limit your beliefs."

I didn't understand. "But—"

"Ah, that's your problem right there," he interrupted. "When you use the word 'but', you are already trying to find a way out. You are giving yourself the 'I can't do that' excuse."

Was it an excuse? I was sure I couldn't do anything that would change the world. Maybe that was his point.

"You can do brilliant things, as can most if they would only try," the man continued. "Lack of self-belief is a major problem. People believe they are not worthy and so don't try. They get too comfortable and sit on the sidelines, watching others be inventive, and then they marvel at them and even cheer them on. It's a pity they don't cheer themselves on. The idols they worship are not so different from themselves. The only difference is they got up off their seat and tried, tried again and tried some more until – wow! They changed their life and that of those around them."

This man made me think. He was right, I still doubted myself. Maybe I suffered from years of conditioning, accepting I wasn't good enough to change anything.

Grandad interrupted my thoughts. "Jack, better you plan to change the world or at least try, rather than accepting a mediocre path."

"That's the spirit," said the man. "Finally, we are getting somewhere. We can't afford to waste our thought bubbles. We need them to land in the right places, where people will take action."

"Can I ask one more question?" I said.

"Ask as many as you want, young man. My job is to help you straighten out some of that spaghetti in your head that you call a brain."

Grandad burst out laughing.

I ignored him. "Are you sure a farm worker like me can change the world?"

"Of course. As soon as a person is born, they have changed the world. But it's what you do to improve the world that's the mark of any human. It happens every day. People in normal jobs invent so many new things. It's not always scientists in laboratories. It's the everyday people who ask, 'How can I improve this?' Whatever you try to improve, do it with love." The man pointed over to the platform extended high in the air. It was almost touching earth. "Go and take your position. Fill your thought bubble with your life-changing ideas and set it free to circulate into the atmosphere. Try to let it land where you believe someone might take your idea and run with it and actually make it happen."

"You've confused me. Are you saying I don't have to make my own idea work?"

"That's correct. By all means try and pursue it if you can. However, if your idea can create massive change for the benefit of others but you don't have time to develop it, then it's better you share it with the wider community. By setting your idea free, you are gifting it to the world so others may catch it. It becomes a roaming thought with the potential to pass through several people's heads and turn into a reality. Sharing in this way helps to progress the world faster."

"Does that mean my idea could be a success and someone else gets the credit?" I asked.

The man winked at Grandad. "Ah, the ego of youth. Refreshing, isn't it?"

Grandad smiled in reply, but held his tongue.

"Young man, if someone had a new idea on how to give every child clean water, would it matter who invented it?"

"I suppose not."

"Improving living conditions for millions is more important than who gets the praise. Do you think those credited for discovering those ideas thought of them first?"

"I suppose so. At least, I thought they did."

"It's true, some will have. But often everyday, normal people have ideas, talk about them, try them, and don't succeed and they end up smashed against rocks somewhere. Other people pick up on their thoughts or their ideas and develop them further. That's why throughout history many inventors began working on the same idea at the same time – it was a shared thought looking for someone to run with it."

"It's interesting that you say that," I admitted. "I had an idea for an extension to a plough. Two years later, I saw my idea on sale at an agricultural show. Someone had a similar thought. I felt robbed."

The man smiled and shook his head. "You shouldn't have. After all, you only thought of an idea. Did you run with it or build the new plough?"

"No. I thought I might at some point."

"That's where the issue is. Farmers are already benefitting because the other inventor took it forward. I'm sorry to say this, but because you took no action, it was a wasted thought, dormant in your head. Thoughts need action to turn them into reality."

I realised this man was right. "As hard as it is for me to agree with you, I believe you are correct."

"I am, young man, and I'm only pointing this out so that the next time you get a similar thought, you will work on it. If you keep thinking and not doing, someone else will pick up on the thought and they'll complete it. Learn to take action."

"I get it. I will act upon it next time."

"That's great." A broad grin stretched across the man's face as he gestured up to the sky. "Look into the atmosphere. There are thousands of incredible and brilliant ideas that have been circulating for years. They've entered many people's heads and yet no one has acted upon them. The opposite happens when an idea lands with two people in different continents, sometimes at the same moment. They might both be working on it simultaneously. Does it matter who thought of it first or gets their name on it if humanity gains?"

"Not really, I suppose." I had never imagined that some of my thoughts could have come from someone else. Someone who had sent them out freely for others to use.

The large man cocked his head and looked at me and Grandad, the wool on his coat fluffed up, making him look even bigger. "I've never seen a pair like you before. Pick a bubble each and head over to the launch platform. Speak clearly into your bubble and make sure your thoughts are inside. The clearer your message, the greater the chance it becomes real. Climb the platform, lean into the atmosphere and set your bubble free." With that, he handed us two clear bubbles. They felt soft and wobbly, and pleasing to the touch.

We thanked the man and carried our bubbles over to the launch platform. A woman showed us a ready-made list of ideas that would improve lives, in case we had none of our own. I thought for a few minutes and then pushed my mouth against my bubble, speaking my idea out loud into it. The bubble turned violet. I put my ear against the sphere and listened to my thought; it came back loud and clear.

Grandad was deep in thought. He paced around under the bottom of the world for twenty minutes while his bubble pulsed like a heartbeat. He was taking his time. I didn't want to disturb him and so sat and watched him from a nearby park bench, holding my bubble. Finally, I saw him whisper into his bubble. He must have spoken for five minutes. The more he spoke, the more his bubble grew in size. He finished and began searching through the crowds for me. I went over and joined him. We headed towards one of the platforms rising high beside our revolving planet Earth.

"You first, Jack," said Grandad.

We climbed the stairs, stopping at the height of ninety feet. The platform continued to rise and push in towards the atmosphere. I felt the coolness of the earth as it drew me in closer. It was humbling as I peered down through the clouds. There was something so fragile about our planet. The platform rose higher, climbing above the equator, my nose now touching the atmosphere. I pushed my fingers through the clouds, dragging lines in them as they moved with the earth. It felt incredible. I pushed my face forward through the atmosphere and felt the ice-cold air. I reached forward with my bubble and waited for my moment.

After a few minutes, I let it go. I prayed for my thoughts to become a reality. I watched my bubble float away from me, spiralling downwards towards the land. As the world turned, my eyes followed my bubble towards America. It settled over New England before disappearing. I hoped my message of becoming a better person would also help others and come true.

Withdrawing my face from the cool atmosphere, I felt happy. Looking around, it was wonderful to see hope on the faces of the people as they released their bubbles. So many wanting to do something that would improve our lives.

"Your turn, Grandad, go on, change the world."

Grandad smiled and shuffled along the platform beside me. "Keep a hold of my belt so I don't fall in."

He stared at the brilliant blue light for a long time as earth spun in front of him. He placed his hand on the outer atmosphere. His eyes were closed as if he were connecting with the pulse of a living, thriving heartbeat. Earth was alive. Humbled, Grandad pushed his hands through the clouds, holding his bubble. He drew in a deep breath and leant forward.

I gripped his belt to stop him falling. I wasn't sure what would happen if I let him go.

Tears flowed down Grandad's cheeks as he observed the beauty of our planet. From where I stood, he looked like some higher power watching over humanity. He pushed his bubble away from his hands. It separated into a hundred mini bubbles. His group of thoughts swirled like a murmuration of starlings, moving in unison as the land passed by below. A storm caught his bubbles, scattering them in every direction.

Grandad smiled, knowing his idea would reach the minds of many. It was too late for him to bring his thoughts to fruition, but not too late to share them. Perhaps one day, someone would run with his idea. Grandad watched the land and seas pass before him for a few minutes more before pulling back from the clouds. He was ice cold. He looked good. We descended the platform in silence.

Grandad hugged me tightly. "Can you believe that, Jack? As I stared at our planet, I felt the most overwhelming love and sadness at the same time. It was so powerful I had to hold myself together from breaking down. What a blessing to witness this."

I could only nod in response. I was working hard at holding back my own tears. I held Grandad in my arms, knowing our time here was ending.

"What a beautiful journey we've taken, Jack. Never would I have believed we'd experience something as profound as watching our beloved earth. I felt so much love for it as if it was part of me and at the same time I felt a great sadness under-standing its fragility. It was way beyond my expectations when we stepped on my bus. If every person saw our planet like this, they wouldn't start wars. They would find beauty and spread more love."

I sighed. "Do you think we will change the world?"

"We already have. Hopefully, at least part of what we released will come true."

"What was your idea, Grandad?"

"Oh, just the wild ravings of a sentimental old man. Even if a small part of my idea worked, it could start a small revolution towards peace. I've always thought it's everyone's job to make the world a better place, more harmonious and help those who need it. I want to bring a little humility to those that have lost it and to leave everything we touch in better condition."

"That sounds good. Is that what was in your bubble?"

"Sort of. Because I never lived my life truly, I've always dreamt of something that would give every young adult the best experience possible. A life they could never afford otherwise. A plan to remove ignorance and bring cultures together and make the world more integrated."

"Is that what you wished for?"

"I called it the trip of a lifetime. Because money clouds everything we do, I thought, why not exchange things? Poverty and wealth are the sickness of our world. What if every young adult could go wherever they wanted? A world with no borders and open to all between the ages of eighteen to twenty-five. Wouldn't that be incredible?"

"What good would that do?"

"It would bring more understanding for everyone. No one need work until they reach twenty-five."

"Twenty-five! That's too old. What would they do?"

"Well, that's the idea I sent off in my bubble."

"Tell me about it."

"Imagine if at eighteen your country gave you a golden card. A World Traveller card. With this card you could travel to any destination, stay at any accommodation, eat well and even work. Wouldn't that be life-changing? You could try every restaurant, every tourist attraction, all for free."

"Sounds like a good plan, Grandad, sign me up."

"Can you imagine how well the youth of our world would integrate with other cultures? Imagine if you could live in France for a few months, perhaps head to Australia before exploring China and then Japan. Anywhere you want to go, all paid for by our governments."

"Sounds amazing, but expensive."

"If the youth of the world lived in many countries and travelled together, hatred and racism would disappear. After seven years, every young adult would have a greater understanding of other cultures. They would have wonderful memories from all the different people they met. They would invite people back to stay with them. That would be my dream. Allow the young to have opportunities like that and they will embrace every other culture. If we want to create a better planet, we need the young to work together for the sake of humanity. We need to be a species that helps itself develop and not separate ourselves as individual countries. We wouldn't allow differences in cultures and skin colour to create division. It would cost very little compared to the money we spend on wars."

"But wouldn't it be dangerous?"

"The world is already a dangerous place. Many world leaders are never content unless they are killing others. We spread hatred and fear in our young about people in other countries. We need a fresh approach with a bold plan."

"I like it, Grandad. Will it happen in my lifetime?"

"I would love it to. I'm feeling optimistic my bubble is on its way. It's been in my head for thirty years. This seems the perfect time to release it. It may never happen, Jack, it's only a dream from an old man."

"You never know, Grandad, dreams can come true. Imagine I could visit anywhere and everywhere in the world I wanted. I'm voting for it and I'll tell everyone it was your idea."

Grandad smiled. "You know, Jack, that man was right. It doesn't matter whose idea we use: if it makes life better for the many, that's all that matters. One day my dream may happen. One day."

We stood and watched the earth spinning, not wanting to leave the most extraordinary view ever.

"Isn't that the most beautiful thing, Jack?"

I stared at earth, trying one last time to take it in, knowing I would never see our world like this again.

"It's incredible, Grandad. There is nothing else like it."

We walked back to the bus in a welcome silence, both feeling exhilarated.

Grandad gave me a hug. "Wherever we go next will never compare with what we've experienced here."

"I agree. Surely not even the Best Seat in the Universe could beat this, Grandad."

"Perhaps," he said and smiled. "Let's head there now."

Ever since we'd arrived in this strange world I had been desperate to find this elusive place, and here we were in the final moments. I looked at the small lavender ticket I had carried throughout the journey. Something within me knew this would be well worth the wait.

Grandad changed the destination board.

THE BEST SEAT IN THE UNIVERSE

THIRTY-SEVEN

THE BEST SEAT IN THE UNIVERSE

"It's now or never, Jack."

"At last, Grandad. I thought you'd changed your mind. I'm so excited. I've wondered since our journey began what this seat looks like and why it's the best in the universe."

Grandad grinned. "When you see it, you'll understand."

"Put your foot down, Grandad. We've been messing around too long in the strangest of places. We should have headed to the Best Seat first."

"Patience, Jack. We had to visit those places to give you a better understanding of life. Each place was necessary. You must have realised that?"

"I did. But now my focus is on finding the Best Seat in the Universe."

"Okay, Jack. Sit back and enjoy the ultimate journey."

The engine of Grandad's bus coughed a few times. A cloud of black smoke poured from the exhaust. He pressed hard on the accelerator but couldn't get power to the engine. His bus crawled along the road for a couple of minutes, then stopped.

He turned the ignition off, and his bus was still. We sat at the roadside, the night sky fading to the darkest blue.

"Why aren't we moving, Grandad? Is something wrong with your bus?"

He laughed. "It would be easier to ask what's not wrong with my bus? I stopped because we've arrived."

I looked out the window, confused. There was nothing but darkness.

"Grandad, we hardly moved. The destination board must be faulty. There's nothing but grass and trees outside. I can't see my seat out there."

"My bus is never wrong. It says we've arrived, so it must be true."

"You've broken down, Grandad."

"It's definitely not broken, Jack. You haven't worked this out yet, have you?"

"I'm not sure what you mean. Am I missing something obvious?"

"I would say so. It's at the tip of your nose and you still can't see it."

"See what?"

"The Best Seat in the Universe, what else? Open your eyes, Jack. Wake up and see what's in front of you."

I wiped the condensation off the glass and peered into the darkness. There was nothing but the outline of trees and hills against the night sky. I sat back and shrugged my shoulders. This was the big moment I'd waited for, and it was a total let-down. This journey had confused me, and I didn't want to discuss it any more. I stared at my reflection in the darkened window, wondering what this was all about.

And then I smiled. "How stupid am I, Grandad? I think I get it."

"Do you, son?"

I nodded. "I believe I've discovered the Best Seat in the Universe, Grandad. It's been staring me in the face the whole time. Would that be right?"

"That depends on what you are seeing."

"I'm seeing my reflection. Could it be that I, I mean me ... could it be that I am the Best Seat in the Universe?"

Grandad took off his driver's hat and smiled. "Well done, Jack. Of course it's you." He reached forward and shook my hand.

Although I'd figured it out, there was a genuine feeling of disappointment within me. "I'm just not sure what it all means."

"It's very simple. You, Jack DeLacey, are now in control of the Best Seat in the Universe. You've been on this journey since the day you were born. Your parents gave you the gift of life for you to do whatever you want with it. You have your body, your thoughts and free will. You can take yourself anywhere you want to go. You can work as hard or as easy as you choose, and you can help yourself or others. Whatever path you take depends on where you drive that bus of yours. You decide who you let on and how you want to live. That's what the Best Seat in the Universe is, and it's yours to take full advantage of."

"So, I own the Best Seat in the Universe."

"Yes, Jack. Your spirit, your soul, whatever you wish to call it, sits inside your body looking out to decide what you are going to do next. Isn't that just the best thing?"

"Why was I chosen and not someone else?"

Grandad laughed. "Jack, it's not only you who gets the best seat, we are all gifted with it. This gift of life allows every person to sit up front of their body, their bus and take control. Each person can do something wonderful or waste their life, it's their choice. It's their life. Will they make the most of what it gives them or waste it and let their opportunity pass them by?"

"I get it. Can I go anywhere, Grandad?"

"Yes, you can. Anywhere you want with no limits. The only restrictions are the ones you place on yourself or if you let others control you."

"I want to run my own life."

"Perfect. It's every person's job to sit in that seat and take their life as far ahead and as high as they dare, no matter what challenges they face. Being born and given a chance at life gives each of us an incredible opportunity."

"Not everyone gets it easy though, Grandad. Remember Lloyd, who was in my class in school? He's blind. That's not exactly the best seat. How can he sit up front and see where he's going?"

"That's true. But when each of us was born, tell me who it was that made the promise our lives would be easy? I don't remember being told it would be easy. Many people face challenges we can't imagine, and we all live with personal issues. It might restrict us, but the right attitude in tough situations will help us overcome our roadblocks. When we are up for the challenge, it's overcoming our issues that reveals the best in us."

"Life seems easier now that I understand how my bus works in getting me to my destination."

"I'm not sure it will be easy, Jack, but try to enjoy it. Every destination will be another achievement. Cross them off and set yourself bigger and harder goals. It's a great way to live because you'll always be moving, always learning. Understanding how your bus works should make it clearer to plan your life."

"It's already changed the way I think, Grandad. I thought I'd be working on the farm for the next fifty years, but now I know I have options. I might still work on the farm, but I'm open to the possibilities of a different life and I'm confident I can make an impact in this world. Do you think that's possible?"

"Of course. You have potential. Start small and build to bigger things. You've sent your bubble into the atmosphere.

Your living thoughts are circling, looking for somewhere to land."

"Mine wasn't anything exciting. I asked to be a better person and help others."

"But that's brilliant, Jack! Imagine if one thousand people receive your thought and take action and become better people. How fantastic would that be?"

A grin broke across my face. "I never thought of it like that."

"Jack, observe your life in all its glory. What you have is a unique and wonderful gift. So many people spoil their own opportunity. Decide what you want to achieve. You're now the driver. Sit proudly up front and go. You are there to change your world. Only you can take decisions in which direction you move. Only you can stop others pointing you the wrong way. It's your seat, your journey and your life, just like I have mine."

"I hope my friends and family will join me on my bus."

"They will, Jack. Work with others. Every time you help someone, you'll enjoy a satisfaction that money can't buy. Give your heart and soul and encourage others, but don't live your life to suit their needs. Ask yourself the one important question of yourself. Does this feel true to me?"

I laughed, thinking over the events of the past few days. "This journey looks like they designed it for me to find my true self."

"I would say so. But not just you: everyone on their own journey should look inwards. They must question life and work on finding their true self. Once they find it, they can take charge of their universe. We need people to be positive and avoid wasting time."

"I agree, Grandad. I'll make you proud of me."

"You already have."

I leaned back in my chair, grinning at my reflection. I'd expected my search for the Best Seat in the Universe to be some golden throne. Now I'd discovered something better. I knew how to shape my destiny. I'd learned where to point my bus and to take one challenge at a time. I understood some people would help me while others would try to hold me back. I would treasure those who played a significant part in my journey. I felt proud to be in charge of the Best Seat in the Universe. My seat, my life and my responsibility to do something great. Thanks to Grandad, I had discovered my place in the universe. Perhaps my job now was to pass this on to others and help them create brilliant lives too.

"I understand the whole 'best seat' thing now, Grandad."

"That's great. I watched the realisation dawning on your face. Where to next, Jack?"

"Can anywhere else be worth going to, now we've been here?"

"This is only the beginning. Now you have to make proper decisions. Consider the exciting discoveries that lie ahead. Time we moved on."

Something was niggling me. "There's one last question you haven't answered."

"What's that?"

"When will I get my bus?"

Grandad smiled. "Now you understand life, it's your job to call on your bus and bring it to life. When you were young, you were a passenger. Now you're a man ready to embrace the challenge. Become a driver who knows where he is heading. Your bus will appear soon."

Grandad changed the destination board.

JOURNEY'S END

"Where's that, Grandad?"

"Where I've been heading since the start of this adventure."

We left the dark forest behind and headed towards a sky of clouds burning red, as the sun dipped down towards the horizon.

THIRTY-EIGHT

JOURNEY'S END

G randad drove towards the top of a hill. His bus spluttered as it tried to scale the steep climb. But the hill proved to be the final straw. We ran out of fuel and came to a dead stop. Black smoke billowed from the exhaust. Grandad let the handbrake off and free-wheeled his bus back down and swung off into a passing place. A signpost pointed towards a scenic viewpoint. His breathing sounded laboured. He dabbed his soaking wet head and face with a hanky. He looked exhausted.

"Are you okay, Grandad?"

"I'm fine, Jack. Although that hill fairly took it out of me. Let's get some fresh air and watch the sunset."

"Okay. I think you could do with a rest."

"I agree."

"Let's do some stargazing. I'll be the storyteller and tell you stories like you used to do with me."

"That sounds good. I would like to do this before I move on to the next level."

"Which level are you talking about?"

"Well, I guess I'm finished with this one and can say truthfully I enjoyed every part. But you know, I'm kind of excited about moving on."

We climbed down the steps of the bus. Grandad was shaky on his feet and held on to my arm. His legs buckled slightly. I told him to take it slowly and held him tight, causing him to laugh.

"What's so funny?" I asked.

"How life changes. I used to hold you to stop you falling and now you're helping me. I believe this is the circle of life."

I lifted two deckchairs from the storage area underneath. A sleek-looking bus sat next to Grandad's. The destination read: YOUR DESTINY. I peered through the window. The bus had digital controls, a TV screen, a toilet and a large air conditioning unit on the ceiling.

"What a beauty, Grandad. It has all the latest technologies. Nothing wrong with your bus, of course, but this is stunning."

"I'm glad you like it. It's yours."

"Mine! What do you mean? It can't be."

"It is, Jack, but let's talk about it later. Trust me when I tell you it's yours. I said your bus would appear when you were ready to take charge of your life, and not a minute before. Well, that time is now."

"My bus is so modern. Why did I get a new one, and yours is, well, it's sort of wrecked?"

He laughed. "It certainly is, isn't it? I'm actually very proud of the way mine looks. When I got my bus, it was like yours, all shiny and bright. It had brand new leather seats and polished chrome – the paintwork was perfect. However, that was a long time ago. What you are witnessing when you look at it now is how hard I've driven my bus. All those bumps and scrapes happened along the way because that's how hard I tackled my life. I lived it to the fullest and have travelled a long way in my seventy-two years."

"You have, Grandad. I don't know anyone who has worked as hard as you."

"Look at my bus closely. Every scar was important. Every mile was a new learning. My peace and love signs have always travelled with me in my heart, while visible for the world to see who I am and what I believe. I can remember most moments of my journey and feel proud. See how my story is unmistakable on my bus? Do the same with yours."

"I'll give it my best shot."

"Good. I believe the worst thing you can do is to arrive at your final destination polished and without a scratch. You want to arrive exhausted and crawling on your hands and knees for the last few feet of your life. Laugh at yourself as your bus falls apart around you. When you finish like that, you'll have earned that gift of life given to you."

A great well of emotion opened up within me as Grandad spoke these words. It was true his bus was barely recognisable. The scars on his bus truly reflected a life well lived.

"Don't play it safe, Jack. Enjoy your journey because this is the only time you get. Take charge with your decisions. Type your goals into your newfangled digital destination board and go towards the places you want to be. Sometimes you'll take wrong turns and find yourself far from where you planned. That's okay too. Enjoy the diversions. Remember, there are no wrong decisions. There's nothing more important than believing in yourself, if you want to fulfil your dreams."

"I will. I'm already lining up my bus stops. I'm ready to go."

"That's good. Come back after we view the sunset. This will be a beautiful moment." Grandad brushed down his clothes and fixed his cuffs and collar. He straightened his back and walked with his head held high. I followed, carrying our deckchairs.

"How do you know the way, Grandad? There's no signs."

"That's the way I like it, Jack. When there are no signs, choose the path that appears true in your heart."

He pushed between gorse bushes and headed downhill towards a breathtaking panoramic viewpoint of the ocean. Birdsong quietened as clouds changed shape against the flaming red backdrop. We could hear the ocean waves drag shingle back and forth on the shore. The sun disappeared beneath the horizon and we watched the moon sail overhead from the comfort of our deckchairs. Grandad took my hand as family and friends arrived, making their way down from where they had travelled on his bus. They sat close by and sang beautiful songs.

Grandad recounted our strange, yet wonderful journey. We laughed until we cried. We watched as stars pierced through the night sky, the Milky Way visible above us.

"Look up at the stars, Grandad. I love how each one gets the chance to shine."

Grandad smiled. "You know, the funny thing is I never think of it as looking up. I've always seen it as looking down into the universe, as if I'm upside down, holding on for dear life. I imagine I'm staring down into space and if the earth should stop spinning, I'd fall off towards the stars."

I laughed at his crazy ways. He always saw things differently.

"When we left, you said you'd take me to the Best Seat in the Universe and now here we are."

"That's true, Jack. And I'm glad you discovered yourself. You've found yourself, your seat in the universe, and like everyone else on this planet, it's your choice to make it the best. Remember the man who gave us our bubble? He told us not to waste it, not to waste your opportunity to do something wonderful. He was right. Jack, it's time to drive your bus towards your dreams and make a difference. Life is a gift. It's yours for the taking."

I shouted towards the sky, "I own the Best Seat in the Universe!"

"As true as you are here, Jack. Your body, your mind, your spirit. I should remind you that this journey I've shown you is purely my viewpoint of life. It's my belief, my universe, and it feels right to me in every way. I believe I am now at one with the universe. I've tried not to tell you how to live your life, merely show you some ways to help you think for yourself before I move on." Grandad reached over and shook my hand. "Thanks for everything, Jack. We had a blast, didn't we?"

I got out of my deckchair and hugged him hard. He looked at me. 'That was like the one Bob gave me,' he said. Tears trickled down his face. We hugged some more. At last he pulled back, still holding my hand. "Jack, my sun has set. It's my time to go. Thank you for being with me for my last moments. I'll miss you, but I promise we will meet again. Here's to us."

"Where are you going, Grandad?"

"To start again. I'll get my new bus, or maybe they'll give me a rocket this time." He laughed.

"Can I talk to you at the big tree?" I whispered, my voice suddenly hoarse.

Grandad nodded and let go of my hand.

He waved as his body floated upwards. I watched for a few minutes until I couldn't see him any more.

Friends and family filled the air with an old spiritual song.

I picked up our chairs and looked up at the sky. The moon shone brightly, surrounded by a coloured halo. The stars flickered.

After a long while I headed back to the clearing and felt a warm feeling, knowing Grandad was okay.

Grandad's bus was in darkness. I looked at his destination board. *OUT OF SERVICE*. It would never drive again. I climbed the stairs, picked up his jacket and hat and had one last look around. I spotted the small ornament of the mouse eating the banana. I put it in my pocket.

I locked the door and walked around his bus for one last view. The peace and love signs were fading. I placed my hand on top of the yin and yang. "Goodbye Grandad." The leaves on the nearby trees rustled as a breeze swept through.

My bus stood at the edge of the road, ablaze with light. I stepped aboard, dazzled by the brightness. The dashboard displayed a fully electronic destination board. I turned the keys and could hardly hear the engine, except for a slight purring noise. I put it into gear and headed onto the highway. How would I find my way home?

I drove for over an hour, but it wasn't the same without Grandad. My mother and father and other family members appeared on my bus. I thought of what Grandad had said about how they would travel along with me as they thought of me. I didn't know where to go. I looked at the street signs and they made no sense. Then I noticed a familiar silvery glowing figure standing at the side of the road. Grandad's guardian angel. She waved me down and smiled as I opened the door.

"Where are you going?" she asked.

"I'm not sure. I thought I would drive around and try my new bus."

"Why not? But your time here is complete, don't you think?"

"I suppose. It looks as if I'm stuck here."

"Then it's time you made your way back home. It's where you should be."

I nodded. "You're right. But I'm lost and can't remember the road out. I came in from the sky."

"Set your destination board to the hospital." She smiled and stepped back into the darkness. I was going to say goodbye, but she'd already disappeared.

How stupid I felt. My first chance to use my bus properly, to take me where I wanted to go and I failed. Grandad was right. Sometimes I'd go in the wrong direction.

I typed the hospital name into the destination board, which illuminated bright orange at the front of my bus. "Take me back," I said.

My bus started along the highway, gathering speed. A bright light appeared in the middle of the road and my bus continued right through it. Lights and stars streamed past me as I accelerated out of control. I held on tight...

And then silence. All I could hear was the alarm of my grandad's heart monitor.

THIRTY-NINE

THE END OF THE END

The nurse pulled my hand from Grandad's and shook me hard to wake me. With the loss of connection, I went from drifting above the room with a heavy jolt back to my earthly body.

A second nurse dragged me away from the bed and sat me outside in the corridor as the emergency team worked hard to save Grandad. It was a strange moment. I watched through the window as they compressed his chest and give him a burst of electricity, but he didn't respond. The line on the monitor remained flat. I wanted to stop them, as I knew he was away on a different trip.

My mother burst into tears as she ran into the room. She grabbed hold of me. "Don't worry, Jack, he'll be fine. They'll save him. You'll see," she cried.

"It's okay, Mum. He's already gone to a better place."

"Watch what you're saying."

"He's already passed away, Mum. I was with him."

"No, don't talk like that. I couldn't cope if anything happened to him."

I knew this was an unusual situation. I'd been with Grandad

at the end of his life and witnessed his death. The only thing I couldn't fathom was the timeline. I believed I was away for at least two days, yet when I returned, his heart monitor was still sounding the alarm. There's no way I could explain this difference. All I knew was I had experienced the most wonderful adventure.

The doctor left Grandad's bedside, approached us and shook his head. "I'm sorry, it's bad news," he said to Mum. "Your dad's heart was too weak to survive. Would you like to sit with him?"

My mother was shaking. I could see her bottom lip trembling as she tried to compose herself. Tears rolled down her cheeks. I squeezed her hand and hugged her. "Everything will be okay, Mum."

Although I felt sad Grandad was no longer with us, it comforted me to know death wasn't a fearful experience. He went towards it willingly, his heart and mind open.

PART THREE
THE REUNION

FORTY

THE BIG TREE

My phone was almost full. I pushed the file up to the cloud to give me more space and to create a backup. I sat back in my chair, looking over the café but seeing nothing. Jack DeLacey was so serious about accuracy in every small detail. It made for a magnificent story. It was most unusual, and in some way, I didn't want to tell the world. I knew other magazines would rewrite their versions and dilute the authenticity and spoil something I found remarkable.

"That's quite a story," I said. "I can hand on heart say I've never heard or read one similar."

"So, you believe me?"

I stared at him. Everything about this man suggested honesty. At no point had I thought he'd embellished his story. He hadn't sensationalised events or tried to convince me. He'd told his story in a matter-of-fact way, as if recounting factual information. "I never thought I would say this to anyone who has ever given my magazine a story, but yes, Jack, I believe you had this experience, a unique experience and it has me questioning a lot of things about my life."

"Will you print it?"

"Of course. The world needs to know that those afraid of death needn't be. You made me feel good knowing it wasn't the darkness peddled to me since childhood."

"That's why I want my story out there in your magazine and online so people can discuss it and stop fearing death. Also, I want others to find their bus and help them through life."

"That's an excellent point. I'm interested to know if you found your bus since you came back? I assume you don't have one now?"

Jack smiled. "It's funny because I do. After Grandad passed away, I told my mother I'd give her a run home on my bus. She thought I'd lost my mind. Only then did I remember it wasn't for transporting me around but to guide me through life."

"Do you use it?"

"Yes, every day. It simplified life for me. A good example would be today's interview. Two weeks ago, I set my destination board and my bus stops as follows:

DESTINATION: TELL MY STORY

First Bus Stop: Find the best magazine for my story

Second Bus Stop: Call the magazine and tell them I have a story

Third Bus Stop: Insist on Frank Cohen or senior reporter

Fourth Bus Stop: Get my story printed or call another magazine

"Setting my destination and working out my bus stops has changed the way I think. I get so much more done."

"I'm very impressed, Jack." I scratched my chin, wondering about how I'd write this up. "And you're still here on the farm. No other ambition after all your talk of changing the world?"

"I'm glad you mentioned that. A couple of years after Grandad passed away, I told my family everything that happened with Grandad and me on our hunt for the Best Seat in the Universe. I couldn't keep this secret to myself any longer, and it all came flooding out. I told them about my need to travel and my uncertainty about taking over and running the farm in the future. And you know what? All my fears of how they would react were completely unfounded. It was strange because my Dad couldn't contain himself and let out a small cheer. He said they wouldn't want to burden me with the farm and were glad I raised my fears. My mum was pure gold. She'd believed I'd always wanted to run the farm and she had kept working hard year after year, thinking she had to make it work for me. When I told her my thoughts, it was as if she had won the relief lottery. She told me how they had both lost so much of their lives, tied down between looking after our crops and livestock, with no holidays or time to themselves. Once they knew how I felt we all agreed to let the farm go. My parents sold it and now they rent Grandad's old cottage back from the new owner. I've been hired as farm manager in charge of the day-to-day running. The new owners are looking to have a healthy work-life balance, so between us it's a team effort now. The best thing is we get paid every month, which wasn't always guaranteed when Mum and Dad owned the farm. I took two years out travelling to Europe and Asia, and I have plans to backpack across Australia next year. I'm back in the job I love, managing the farm, but as a family we no longer have the lifetime responsibility or a great-great-grandfather looking over our shoulders. That biggest single pressure has been removed."

"That's incredible, Jack. You really did get what you wanted. I'm very impressed. Seems like a new start for the whole family?"

"It is, and I'd say we are all happier now. My mum has never looked so good with all the stress now gone and I have big plans for my future."

"It sounds like it's worked out well for everyone."

"It has I'm glad to say. Tell me do you need anything else regarding my story, Frank?"

"Would it be possible for me to take some photographs of you?"

"Sure. Why don't we head out to the farm and take some in the fields? I can show you the big tree."

"I'd like that very much. Not sure I'll be able to climb it at my age, but I'd like to see this famous big tree."

"Anyone can climb this tree. The large branches make it so easy to climb each level."

We headed over to the farm, and Jack gave me a few pictures of his Grandad. I wished I'd met this man, a genuine character who left so many memorable moments behind him. The similarities between him and Jack were uncanny. As we walked through the fields, I felt like a living character in his story. Jack's descriptions were accurate. The tree was everything he described, and it commanded attention with its impressive size against the landscape. We sat in its shade and watched the dragonflies fly above the water. I let Jack walk about while I shot some photos with my camera. I felt as if I'd found the story of the century. After my career of forty years, I'd never thought I'd find a story that would have such an impact on me.

I balanced my camera on a branch and set the timer. It took a photo of us both standing under the tree. I climbed up to the hollowed area and Jack went higher to take my photo from above. It was cool in the shaded area. Something pressed hard on my back. I reached behind and grabbed the offending object, thinking it was part of a branch. I opened my palm to find I was holding a tiny carved mouse eating a banana.

"Hey, Jack, didn't you tell me about this?"

He nodded. "It was in my pocket when I returned. I don't understand how it's possible."

"What's it made of?"

"That's funny you should ask. No one I know can identify it. Someone suggested it could be carved from a meteorite."

It did feel strange. I didn't want to leave. I shook Jack's hand and thanked him for sharing his story.

Jack scratched his head, regarding me with an odd look on his face.

"What is it, Jack?"

"I was thinking maybe you should turn on your phone again to record. There's one last part of the story I haven't mentioned."

I stared at him. "You're joking with me, aren't you?"

He shook his head. "No, I have one more thing."

I struggled to think what Jack could have missed. His account sounded complete to me and my concern was he would say something that would inadvertently spoil a perfect story. "Okay, Jack, let's hear this last part. Can you remember where in the story it belongs?"

"Of course. I forgot to tell you the ending."

"The ending? What could have happened after your Grandad passed away?"

"You'll understand once I explain."

I pulled my phone from my pocket and switched it back on. I settled back against the tree.

Jack picked a piece of grass and chewed on it. He continued his story.

FORTY-ONE

SCATTERING OF ASHES

I was ready to honour Grandad's last request.

I left before midnight. My parents were asleep, and I knew I'd be back before sunrise, so they wouldn't notice I'd been out. I filled my backpack with snacks and water and wrapped a heavy tin decorated with angels inside my blanket. I closed the front door and headed into the night. I walked through the fields listening to the silence broken only by the odd scurrying sound.

I felt free with the breeze blowing through my hair. I nodded to Stan the scarecrow and vaulted the fence into the next field. Looking back towards the hill, I lost sight of my house in the darkness. The fields were at their best, shimmering in the moonlight, as the wind swayed the crops back and forth. An owl dropped like a stone into a clearing, picking up a field mouse with clinical accuracy. Farmhouses with their lights still burning were dotted across the landscape.

The silhouette of the big tree stood out against the night sky. I patted the trunk like I'd done all my life. Five memorised steps took me into the hollowed area known as the den. I lay there thinking about my grandad and all he'd taught me. I thought back on our adventure, our crazy bus journey and how visiting the afterlife had transformed my way of life.

I settled into a dream state, staring out at the stars. I was sure Grandad was shining brightly somewhere amongst them while keeping an eye out for me. More stars appeared as my eyes adjusted, while the moon reflected like a spotlight on the winding river below.

Hunger pangs unsettled me. I pulled my sandwich and a water flask from my backpack. After a while, I spoke out loud.

"Grandad, you said this is your favourite place in the entire universe. Are you here with me now? Talk to me or give me a sign."

The leaves rustled in the breeze. Was it a sign?

"I'm going to do it now, Grandad. Your last request."

I pulled the towel from my backpack and unwrapped the silver tin. It was heavy. I prised open the lid, climbed up higher and shimmied along the thick branch, sprinkling Grandad's ashes back and forth, watching as they floated downwards like a little snowstorm.

I dropped down and spread the remaining ashes around the base of the tree.

"You're home now, Grandad. You'll become part of this tree and live forever. Rest in peace. I miss you."

I climbed back into the den and covered myself over with my blanket. Grandad was at peace. I thought of the fun times we'd spent together. Even as a boy he'd treated me like an adult. He let me drive tractors from eleven years old.

I began to drift off. I wrapped my blanket around my shoulders and settled down. I'd head home early in the morning and be home before anyone missed me. The hollow was comfortable, and I dozed.

I wasn't sure what brought me out of my sleep. I listened. A twig cracked and my body froze. Maybe it was a stray animal feeding below. I couldn't see the hands on my watch. I must have slept about an hour. My heart sounded like it was bursting through my chest. I tried to cover it up to quieten it and peered down from the den.

Two shadowy teenage figures passed below, speaking in hushed voices. Craning my neck to get a better view, I noticed a fire ablaze near a small copse of trees, tended by two adults. Poachers wouldn't draw attention to themselves, I told myself. I assumed they must be campers.

I drew back and remained still, not wanting to scare the teenagers and hoping they would move on. If they climbed the tree, they would get the fright of their lives.

A boy spoke first. "So, this is the famous tree."

"Gran was right when she said the tree was huge," said a girl's voice.

"Compared with the other trees, it's massive. I wonder what all the white dust is? Strange."

"Yeah, what is that?"

I watched as the boy ran his fingers through Grandad's ashes that had landed on the branch.

"Don't touch it, it might be poisonous!"

Peering out again, I saw the boy wipe his hands on the grass. "Do you think Gran and Grandpa will visit the tree tonight?" he said.

"No, they're setting up camp. They said they'll wait till morning. Why they want this trip down memory lane, I don't know. I'm not sure I'd want to relive a strange man coming out of the darkness and scaring the life out of me. I think that's why Gran said she'd leave it for now."

"You and Gran are scared of your own shadows. I wouldn't be frightened. Why we had to travel halfway around the world on a stupid spiritual journey, I can't understand it. Why travel this far to visit a tree when theme parks with rollercoasters are nearby?"

"Theme parks? Wash your mouth out! You've heard what Grandpa says: 'Who needs theme parks when Mother Nature provides all the real experiences of the world...' Boring, let me at them."

They both laughed.

My body was trembling. I couldn't control my thinking. This couldn't be happening, could it? Somehow I knew they were talking about Grandad. The kids sounded English. Could the couple at the fire possibly be...

I leaned out of the hollow and saw the children sitting astride the lower branch. I cleared my throat. "Excuse me, are your grandparents called Bob and Joan?"

The girl froze while the boy jumped down from the branch and ran screaming towards their camp. A second later she followed at great speed behind him.

I heard the commotion at the campsite and thought it best to leave before they returned.

As I dropped onto the branch below, it was too late. A man caught me in the beam of his flashlight, the three others following behind him. I climbed back up into the hollow to provide some distance between us. The torch's beam landed on my face.

"What did you say to scare my grandkids?"

Although blinded by the light, I could tell they were all staring at me. "Nothing," I said.

"It wasn't nothing. You scared the life out of them. Tell me or I'm coming up after you."

The situation seemed ridiculous. "I asked if your names were Bob and Joan."

"What?" said the man. I saw him glance at his wife, who was shaking. "How is it possible you could ask such a question?"

"I thought you may be from the past."

"You're too young to be from our past, son. We've not been here for at least thirty years. Unless I'm mistaken, you're about eighteen."

"Twenty-one. But you have been here before? You're also from England, so I would guess your names are Bob and Joan."

The man laughed. "Do you think every couple from England has those names? What's really going on here?"

Something in his laughter reassured me and I dropped down from my vantage point. The man stared at me without moving. The teenagers looked shocked. It was the woman who surprised me. She came forward and took me by the shoulders.

"Thirty years ago, we had a strange encounter here. We return and you come out of the darkness and know our names. This is too weird for words. What's happening at this place, Bob?"

"Leave it, Joan. There's a simple explanation. Who are you, son?"

"I'm the grandson of the man you met before. My name is Jack."

"How do you know we met someone? Why are you here in the dark?"

"I'm not sure you'll believe me, and the reason is stranger than you could ever imagine."

"Try me."

"Okay, if you insist."

And so I told them about how Grandad had told me about their meeting all those years ago, and what they did, changing his life with their different ways of thinking.

"I can't believe your grandfather's still alive," Joan exclaimed. "That's fantastic! We've been desperate to find him. How crazy it is that we've met you and you're related to him."

"Not crazy. Meant to be." I took a deep breath. "My

Grandad died last month. That's why I was here tonight. I came down to spread his ashes around the tree."

The teenagers looked horrified and brushed themselves down, before running back to their camp.

"How sad," Joan said. There were tears in her eyes. "We're sorry for your loss. What a wonderful man. Our paths crossed for the briefest period, but he had a significant impact on us and we shared a night so memorable."

"He felt the same way, but it was you who changed his life forever. You taught him so much. He left you with his head bursting with new ideas. He bought the books you recommended and changed his way of life."

They invited me over to their campfire, where we settled down with some tea. Their grandkids stayed in their motorhome, probably too freaked out to come out.

"No VW camper van this time?" I asked.

"Ah, we laid old Bessie to rest many years ago. She served us well. We thought of hiring one, but back then it was only me and Joan, we were young and slim." Bob patted his bulging stomach with a smile. "We're a tad larger now, plus we brought the grandkids. It would've been a squeeze." He held up his car keys. Dangling from his key chain was a VW sign, and a beautiful enamelled yin and yang. "Can't live without it," he said. "Always focus on the balance of life."

I smiled. Everything about Bob and Joan felt true. They radiated warmth unlike anyone else I'd ever met. I loved their casual acceptance of this miracle. "Grandad explained the sign to me. I've changed my life already."

"Good for you. Try to live by it and understand the balance. When you live by the sign in a balanced way, it will guide you through dark times. When you understand everything has its opposite, life becomes easier."

"Isn't this strange?" said Joan. "We were wanderers with no

firm roots. We travelled the world and loved our freedom ... until we met your grandfather and he told us all about his family, how close-knit his community was and how everyone helped each other. We wanted a similar life. We wanted a place to call home and put down roots. We travelled back to England excited, bought a plot of land and built our home. We involved ourselves in the community and worked hard to help others. We thought of everything that your Grandad taught us, and our lives undoubtedly changed for the better. To us, meeting someone that honest and kind-hearted was refreshing. His words were powerful, and we've never looked back."

Bob put a hand on her arm. "Joan, do you know where we put the photographs?"

She nodded, and stepped into the motorhome, returning with a photograph album. She flipped through until she found a page, then held out the album to me.

The tree was bigger now. Twenty foot taller perhaps, but the main branches weren't that different.

Joan turned the page. There was a photo of her and a much younger-looking Bob dressed in floral clothes, beads and kaftan, standing next to a VW van decorated with some familiar hippie artwork. "Your grandad took this picture of us."

I beamed from ear to ear. "That's a good one. Did you take any of him?"

Joan turned the page of the album to show a photo of Bob standing with Grandad beside the camper van. "We only have this one picture of him. We brought it with us to find the tree and thought how amazing it would be if we could meet up with him again. We weren't sure we would find this area again, but even in the dim light, this tree stood out in the distance."

How strange this all seemed. I marvelled at how they'd held Grandad up as the person who changed their lives, while all along he'd seen them as the catalyst for his change.

We sat for the next few hours, telling stories, and I told them all about the bus journey.

"That was one hell of a trip you shared," Bob said when I'd finished. "I would've paid a lot of money to go on that trip, especially the experience of seeing earth up close. What an adventure that would be."

That's what I loved about them most. They never doubted whether I had been on a trip; they never asked if I was sure or suggested it was a dream. Instead they listened and answered back with full trust in my words.

The sun came up. It was time for me to leave. They both hugged me, and I invited them to our house for breakfast. They were delighted with the invite, but said they had a full schedule planned and would try and drop in on their way back.

"It was our pleasure meeting you, Jack," Bob said. "We came to remind ourselves of our night with your Grandad. We never thought we'd have a repeat experience with his grandson."

"I only wish we'd visited months ago and met with him once again," Joan added.

"Me too. He would have loved this." I gave them both another hug. "Now I'd better head home before my mother sends out a search party."

As I left, the morning sun turned the fields of corn a golden orange colour. Birds scattered as I waded through the tall grass. I assumed my euphoria matched how Grandad had felt, many years earlier. To this day I remain convinced the big tree is an ancient soul that brought us all together.

"That's my story complete, Frank. What do you think?"

FORTY-TWO

A BETTER LIFE

I stopped my recorder and shook Jack's hand.

"Incredible. You caught me out with that ending. To think you met with Bob and Joan! I never saw that coming. How wonderful. I hope you swapped addresses?"

Jack reached into his pocket and brought out photos of them standing together at the big tree and the original photo of Bob, Joan and Grandad taken many years ago at the same spot.

"Can I get a copy of these for the story?" I asked him.

"Sure. I'm looking forward to see how you tell my story."

So was I. "Me too. What impact would you like it to have, Jack?"

"I would love people to discover their buses and head towards a better life. Also, I don't want them to fear death, because I'm positive it will be a beautiful moment, with nothing to be frightened of."

As we left the site of the enormous tree and climbed back up the hill, my editorial brain kicked in and I began to think about my magazine and its title. What Jack had shared with me fitted every criteria in being weird, wonderful and true. For all the stories we had printed, certainly most were weird, many of them were wonderful but I think this was the first story I can honestly say that I believed to be true.

As we reached the brow of the hill I glanced back for one last look. The sunlight from behind the foliage of the big tree danced as the leaves rustled in the breeze. The sun's rays burst through, giving the tree a golden aura against the backdrop of the landscape. I watched, mesmerised for a few moments. Something truly spiritual was unfolding in front of my eyes and I wish I could put my finger on it. All I was sure of was this ancient tree was central to all that had happened.

FRANK COHEN
   Editor, *Weird, Wonderful, True*

THE END

THE BEST SEAT IN THE UNIVERSE - A POEM

One single moment in time brought you life and now you can share in this paradise.
This life, gifted freely to you, is yours to take and run hard like the wind in any or all directions, because this is your precious space and time.

The communities you know, those you walk and live amongst, have fed and shaped you to who you are.
But now you must sculpt your own form into something accept-able that you dream or desire to be, and not be a product of others bias

You stand untethered to the edge of this world, a playground within your universe.
Realise this can't be anything other than a solo journey for you, even though others may join your tribe and walk part of the way with you, regardless, you remain on a solo flight because we are never anything other than individuals

There is nothing you can possess of more value than your ability

to give to others, your time, your wisdom, your skills and a
shoulder to lean or cry on because giving is something everyone
can do, freely
And what for yourself, what prize can you give that's big
enough to satisfy your inner yearnings.
Nothing less fitting than a mission to help humanity even if only
in the smallest way

It was you who were gifted this treasure of life, your inner being,
your soul, the Best Seat in the Universe
So don't waste your unique opportunity,
Go forward in that body you wear, regardless of shape, size or
colour and prove you were a worthy recipient of life.

Make the most of your unique gift and try to change the world
for the better at least before you take your final breath in this life

Your last moment will be beautiful, euphoric and blissful, and
nothing else is left for you to do except take an effortless step
towards your next place of adventure in paradise

Grahame Anderson - June 2021

CAN YOU HELP ME, PLEASE?

If you enjoyed this book, I would appreciate your help. The best way you can help to promote an aspiring writer like me is by giving my book a review.

I don't have an extensive following, so every review is like gold dust. I'm not asking for a tremendous review, just a sincere account of what you took from reading this book. Fair reviews can bring this book to the attention of like-minded readers, and hopefully they, too, will enjoy my story.

Leaving a review will only take a few minutes of your time, and you can do so on the book's page of whatever store you bought this from. You can find me by searching *Grahame Anderson, The Best Seat in the Universe*.

Thank you in advance and please look out for my future publications. I still have many stories to tell.

Grahame Anderson, June 2021

ABOUT THE AUTHOR

Grahame Anderson is the author of *The Best Seat in the Universe*, *Grahame Anderson's Short Stories and Poems* and *The Lighthouse Keepers*.

You can keep up to date with Grahame or read a selection of short stories and poems for free at:

www.grahameanderson.co.uk

Contact Grahame :
    www.facebook.com/GrahameAnderson
    www.instagram.com/grahameanderson

Grahame lives with his wife, Brenda, and two sons on the West Coast of Scotland. He has worked in print, media and the web for over forty years. When not writing, he enjoys walking, listening to podcasts and reading.

ACKNOWLEDGMENTS

Thanks to the love of my life, my wife, Brenda. I want to thank her for the encouragement to keep going through the many iterations of this book. Without her support, this book would not have been possible.

Thanks to Roan and Luke for their insights through many a midnight discussion. For the listening to and singing out loud to *Abbey Road*, drinking a few bottles of Corona and Peroni and being blessed with a once in a lifetime opportunity to have quality time together because of lockdown. This period in time certainly was a double-edged sword, but I'm pleased we took full advantage of this, had so much fun and grew together.

A special mention and thank you to my editor, Bryony Sutherland. A professional through and through, whose understanding and reshaping of this book brought it to a state that made me feel proud to have written such a story. Her insight of story, characters, continuity and how to improve on these is an unbelievable skill. Her ability is a wonder of the editing process that remains a mystery to me. All I can do is thank her, feel glad that she's on my team and look forward to working with her on upcoming projects.

Thanks to my family, Blair, Clive and Audrey, for not being too embarrassed about what I might write. My friends, Brian and Morag, Robert and Gwyneth, John and Avril, Tommy and Maureen and last but not least, Danny and Anne. Great friends who all keep quiet and just let me get on with it.

The poet John Donne once said no man is an island, and that's true in the writing world. Big thanks to the members of Greenock Writers' Club and to the Scottish Association of Writers, whose members inspire me in so many ways when I read the incredible work many of them produce.

My beta readers, who worked through an early version giving valuable feedback: Barry and Lynne McGugan, Helen Heffernan, Evelyn Davie, Audrey Murray, Mhairi Gilchrist, Tommy McIntosh, Clive, Audrey, Blair, Brenda, Roan. Alan and Mena Steele for their encouragement; Harry Young for patiently listening and playing devil's advocate on different chapters; Sandy Draper for a very, very early edit. Chris Hanlon, Paul Connelly, Ian Hart and David Paterson for giving me business insights I would never have worked out by myself, not forgetting Jason Moore, salesman extraordinaire. Lastly, to everyone else on my journey who inspired me through their thoughts and actions. If I've missed anyone I'm sorry – please let me know. As is the case with modern technology, I can update this part of the book quickly.

Thank you.
    Peace and Love,
    Grahame

THE LIGHTHOUSE KEEPERS

This gentle story follows Max Bruford, an aspiring young music student torn between his parents' opposing views of his future. When he meets two mysterious lighthouse keepers, they give him something magical to help him achieve his goals. Forty years later, he returns and asks them to explain their gift. Their answer is not what he expected.

Many of us suffer from imposter syndrome, the modern label for self-doubt. This lack of self-belief can limit your ambition and take away opportunities you secretly strive for but won't explore for fear of failure.

This book is about self-belief. It may help you reflect on where you are in life and push you forward, towards the person you always wanted to be. Take a leap of faith: every new beginning starts with the first step.

The Lighthouse Keepers, a heart-warming tale about a young man's aim to be the best musician in the world, will help you reflect on your dreams and ambitions. It will give you hours of pleasure and hopefully the message will last you a lifetime.

THE BEST SEAT IN THE UNIVERSE ONLINE

Hopefully, after reading this book, something will have struck a chord. Please visit my website for updates on my writing. I expect to run some online courses based on *The Best Seat in the Universe* at www.bestseatintheuniverse.com.

In my courses, I will dive deep to explain each chapter and explore how you can apply its message to help you. In the chapters of the book I often wanted to give additional examples of how to help in different situations, however, space was always a limitation, therefore I have added these examples into the courses. Different ideas can strike a chord with people in different ways.

This website should be live at the time of publishing. The courses should be available late 2021.

Sign up for my newsletter at www.grahameanderson.com.